The Flatdweller's Companion

A HANDBOOK FOR CITY SURVIVAL

ELGY GILLESPIE

Torc Books

First published in 1972

Torc Books
Published by Gill and Macmillan Ltd.
2 Belvedere Place
Dublin 1
and in London through association with the
Macmillan
Group of Publishing Companies

7171 0636 5

Cover designed by Hilliard Hayden

Printing history
5 4 3 2 1

Printed and bound in the Republic of Ireland by
Cahill & Co. Limited Dublin 8

DEDICATION

I WROTE this book before, during and after looking for places to live myself. Not that I ever learnt from my mistakes. On the contrary, I make them bigger and better as time goes on and home follows home. But I did the fieldwork myself all right.

So I'm dedicating this book to Jo, Noeleen, Arthur, Fran, Sara, Ros, Mrs Fleming, Sam, John, Evelyn, Oliver, William, Philippa, Phil and everyone else who ever gave me a bed or a floor to stay on when for one reason or another I had nowhere else. The best I can wish for them is that they never have to do it again.

ACKNOWLEDGEMENT

I'D LIKE to thank the doctors, lawyers, cooks, gardeners, carpenters, electricians and taxi-drivers who helped me compile the information in this book, and added advice. And specially Joan, Maire and Gus who with all my working colleagues held me together while I wrote it. Theodora Fitzgibbon and Nuala Donelan are writing books of their own. The rules of their professions prevent me from naming my other helpers in print.

CONTENTS

INTRODUCTION

THIS book is intended as a survival kit for citydwellers: a compendium of all the odds and ends of information people usually ask each other or pick up through hard experience. Nobody teaches you how to find places to live or how to change plugs and track down launderettes. Most of us sink for long periods until we can swim—or manage some kind of dogpaddle. So I hope to help people living on their own in the city—students, school-leavers and young couples—to learn a bit about Dublin and other cities.

Addresses and telephone numbers, except in the Appendixes, always apply to Dublin unless I say otherwise.

1

A ROOF OVER YOUR HEAD

So you've left home, you're in the city and you want a flat. Or a room. Anything.

There are some 40,000 flats and bedsitters officially in Dublin, and many many more unofficially. But the population of the city is teetering on the million mark, so there aren't enough to go round. Dublin was never meant to hold a third of the country's population; but as more people leave the countryside and less leave the country, the need for accommodation rises. And the same goes for the other cities of the 32 counties, bulging at their little eighteenth- and nineteenth-century seams. And a look at Hollyfield or Mountpleasant Buildings will show you that somebody gets the raw deal in this imbalance.

Everybody is looking for them: that's why Dublin flats are nearly as expensive as those of London and New York now—it's a sellers' market.

Looking for a flat is a depressing business. The best ones are inherited from friends, passed lovingly down the line over the years. If you know other flatdwellers, you can keep a lookout and take over their flats when they leave. It is sometimes a good ploy to put up with a so-so place for a short time if you know someone about to move out of the Flat of your Dreams. Or take temporary digs in Clontarf or Churchtown with hearty fried breakfasts thrown in to keep you going while you find a foothold; these are advertised under 'Accommodation' in the evening papers, and generally mean long and lonely bus-rides to and from the city and rules about how deep your bathwater should be.

If you have just arrived in Dublin and don't know anyone who can put you up, here are some places you can stay while you're looking.

Boys : you can stay the odd night—(the official maximum is three, but in the winter months the wardens may use their own discretion) in the Youth Hostels at 39 Mountjoy Square and 78 Morehampton Road. You need to be a member of An Oige, which costs £1.50 if you are over 21 years of age, £1 if you are 16-20 and 50p in the unlikely event of your being under sixteen. From October to May, when the Mountjoy Square branch is closed, the Morehampton Road branch is open only for Friday and Sunday nights. In summer both are open full time but are clogged up with foreign hitch-hikers groaning under the weight of their rucksacks. You book by paying cash for a voucher, or by going there at 5 pm when the hostels open. It costs you 40p a night if you are over 21, 35p for 18-20, 30p for 16-17, and 20p should you be under 16; so it's by far the cheapest temporary accommodation, but bear in mind that it's strictly speaking for student tourists. There's an extra charge of 5p for a sheet and you are expected to fold your blankets and do your own cooking. You have to be in by 11 pm (lights out by 11.30) and out by 10 am. Ring to check before you go: 39 Mountjoy Square, tel: 45734, 78 Morehampton Road, tel: 680325. There is another cheap night's sleep, if you aren't too fussy, at the Iveagh Hostel in Old Bull Alley (beside St Patrick's Cathedral). It takes in men only for 40p, and is open from 7 pm–9.30 am. De luxe (with a reading lamp, and the wash-house on the same floor) is 48p, tel: 753247.

Overseas students can try Koinonia House at 60 Harcourt Street. Rates are £1.50 a night or £8.25 a week for full board and the telephone number is 752013; they are booked out, though, very soon after the academic year has begun in October.

2

The Salvation Army Men's Hostel in York Street (tel: 754039) will give you a bed and breakfast for 35p—as will (on more spartan lines) Dublin Corporation Lodging House in Benburb Street (tel: 770689) for 5p a night if you're broke. The Simon Community at 9 Sarsfield Quay by Kingsbridge will also take you in if you are genuinely skint. Again, it is run by committed people for the down and out. If they have no room they will send you to the Morning Star hostel which costs 20p per night.

The **girls'** YWCAs are usually full during the university term times, but are comfy; a more permanent proposition. The branch at 64 Lower Baggot Street costs upwards of £4 per week for a bed in a double room, tel: 66273. The Radcliffe Hall YWCA in St John's Road, Sandymount, is for long-term residents and costs £6 plus for a single room, tel: 693283.

If these are full, girls can try the *Girls' Friendly Society* at 34 St Stephen's Green, tel: 62933. Rates are £6.50-£7 per week and night keys are given. Transistors must be off by 11.15 pm but otherwise it is relatively rule-free.

Students in Trinity College can obtain lists of approved lodgings and flats or they can apply for rooms in College, in the Cumberland Apartments and in Trinity Hall. Consult the Registrar of Chambers at Trinity College, Dublin 2, for further information.

Girls at UCD can also apply for places at a number of hostels. They are pretty freedom-restricting; but good if you are very young and scared of the big bad city. The Deans of Residence will supply lists of approved hostels and lodgings if you ask for them.

But for the first few nights while you are hunting for a long-term flat, a small bed-and-breakfast place will probably be your best bet. There are many reasonably cheap ones in the Amiens Street area : they vary from 75p-£1.50 a night, breakfast included, and from plain-but-decent to real old kips. (Don't leave anything valuable in your rooms.) You can look them up in the Golden-Pages Directory and phone them to save a long, sad trek from door to door.

If you are new to Dublin and don't know anyone yet, don't start looking for a single bedsitter. You will implode from loneliness; anything is better, even sharing with someone who has the same effect on you as silver paper on a tooth filling. The newspapers carry ads from flatdwellers looking for people to share with : particularly the *Irish Times* and again the evening papers— the *Evening Press* and *Evening Herald*. You can insert an ad yourself looking for others to take a flat together.

Seasoned flat-hunters agree that Saturdays are the best days to get the papers for accommodation columns, Sundays are the best days to go looking, and spring and summer are the best times of year. Unquestionably September-October are the worst times, because that is when the students and school-leavers arrive in their homeless thousands.

Prepare for a frenzied week or two. The best method is to put on your most sober (landlord-impressing) clothes and take a fistful of twopenny pieces along for the telephone. The best paper for 'Flats Vacant' is the *Evening Press.* If you get to their offices on Burgh Quay at 1.45 pm when the first edition rolls off the press, you can get a look-in half an hour before the rest of the city.

Scan the last-but-one pages under 'Flats and Accommodation' and ring the ones that appeal to you. Here is a glossary of terms :

s/c : self-contained. Means you have your own bathroom, kitchen and front-door.

hall flat : the one beside the front door. Means you hear all the other tenants thunder in and out at morning and night.

4

American kitchen : sink and cooker—probably a Baby Belling—are part of the open-plan living area.

Kitchenette : sink and hot-plate grill without an oven —are crammed into a corner of the main room.

Sleeps four : unless it states how many rooms, it probably means the bedroom is crammed shoulder-to-shoulder and end-to-end with mattresses.

Storage heating : on meter, and you pay. Expensive.

Suit two ladies : for some reason landladies are adamant about what sex they want their tenants to be when they express a preference. So if you're the wrong one, don't bother.

Make hotfoot for the nearest pub telephone—if you can't use a private phone—and try all the possibles *immediately* because you can be sure an army of likewise soberly-dressed people with fistfuls of twopenny pieces are descending on other city-centre telephones.

The *Evening Herald* comes out in O'Connell Street around the same time as the *Evening Press*. The *Irish Times* tends to have pricey flats. The *Independent* and the *Irish Press* also have 'Flats to Let' columns with occasional golden finds.

If the advertisement says to go round at a certain time, go a bit early. Unless you can con someone with a car into taking you around, it's going to be pretty hectic tearing from Harold's Cross to Phibsboro'. Beg, borrow or steal enough money to put down as a deposit in case you should stumble onto a really good one: at least £20. And get a receipt if you use it.

Areas. Everything on the south side costs more than the north side, and Ballsbridge addresses will be the most expensive of all. It is becoming usual now to be asked

£20 per week for an all-electric furnished flat in Dublin 4, with sitting room, bedroom, kitchen, bathroom and tasteful reproduction of a foaming seascape thrown in. In traditional bedsitter land—Pembroke Road, Wellington Road, Waterloo Road, Raglan Road, Morehampton Road, Percy Place, Herbert Place, Fitzwilliam Square and Upper Leeson Street—you can be asked from £5 up to a cool £10 a week for a single bedsitter, depending on the state the room is in. And by the time this book is printed it will probably have gone up.

But you should still find a two-roomed self-contained flat for £10 per week without too much difficulty in Rathmines, Sandymount, Ranelagh, Rathgar or the South Circular Road. And with a bit of luck it can be less. Three rooms are rarer and tend to hover around £15 per week. They seem to go up by a pound or so a year: in '68 nice flats seemed to be £8 per week or thereabouts. Note: landlords charge per bed, rather than by room. So 'for four girls' may mean one bedroom almost completely crammed out with beds.

It's a very different story on the north side. The odd geographical snobbery of Dubliners means that a smallish room with a sink in it and a view of, say, a brick wall can be as low as £2.50 or £3 in Drumcondra or the North Circular Road. A double bedsitter or two-roomed flat will be around £5-£8 per week. Sutton and Clontarf are 'nicer' areas, and will cost a little more even though they are farther out. Fairview is usually in between.

If you are a married couple, and particularly if you have children, you will find the going much harder. At a recent, informal count only one Dublin landlady in two hundred would take couples with young babies. Students will also find it difficult.

The odd white lie is therefore necessary; if you are a shorthand typist you can say you are a secretary; if you are a student nurse you can say you are qualified; if you are a first-year student you can say you are post-graduate. And smile winningly.

Beware of racketeering agencies. At the time of writing there are five of these agencies in operation in the city; they move about fairly often and change their names as well. Since they were exposed by Liam O Cuanaigh in the *Press* and Kerry McCarthy and Janet Martin in the *Independent,* the papers have refused to carry their advertisements. But most get round this by putting an anonymous and delectable ad in, such as 'City centre, two-roomed self-contained hall-flat semi-furnished, suitable for couple with child', and then tag their own phone number on the end. The irresistible flat is a figment of their imagination, but in this way they lure the most despairing flat-seekers to their offices. They then charge them up to £4 on the spot, and send them in droves to the same place. Generally their addresses are pulled from the day's evening papers, and the landlords sometimes are not even aware the seekers are sent from these agencies. Getting your money back again is tough. Which isn't to say that some good flats have not been found via agencies. If you decide to try them, do not give them any money without finding the flat or room you want.

Unfurnished flats are very rare these days, for the simple reason that it is very hard to get someone out of an unfurnished letting, once in. They are rarely adver-tised; if you want one it is best to put an ad in for one yourself or consult the lists of unfurnished accommoda-tion prepared by some of the larger estate agents, such as North's or Lisney's. The prices are very much the same as for furnished flats, and the advantages are great because you will be able to acquire your own furniture to put in the flat—and scratch it as much as you like.

7

They invariably come with a lease attached, since only people who want to stay for a couple of years or more require them. Generally if a landlord can supply a bed and a kitchen table and an ashtray and call a flat furnished he will, these days, because his own security is then greater.

Other ways of finding flats

Inserting an ad yourself. The girls in the newspaper front offices say that the most successful ads are the most specific. If you say exactly how many rooms you want, and pin down the area along with other requirements and the sort of price-range you want you will tend to get more replies. For instance 'teacher wants single room with bathroom, telephone essential, Terenure-Rathgar, £6 pw' gives a future landlord more description to go on than 'required, bedsitter; any area considered'. If you can give a phone number, or persuade somebody to take messages for you, it will be more hopeful than a box number. The cost of putting in ads can usually be found in the newspaper advertisement columns.

Public notice boards. Some small paper shops put cards in their windows offering or asking for accommodation. Cora's in Ranelagh Road (just past the junction with the Appian Way) and local small post offices will take them. Trinity has cards asking for people to share or sub-let flats in the Regent House gateway. And there are notice boards both at Belfield and at Earlsfort Terrace which are used for the same purpose by UCD students.

Asking. I know somebody who found a three-roomed top-floor flat on the quays for £4 per week by asking in a sweet-shop nearby. You will often as not be rebuffed, but if you ask very nicely and look your most wholesome, who knows?

8

Auctioneers. Unlike the agencies, these charge land-lords instead of tenants (usually about $2\frac{1}{2}$ per cent of the year's rent). Lisney & Sons, 23 St Stephen's Green, tel: 64471, North & Co., 54 Dame Street, tel: 774721, Ken Walters, 4 Pembroke Park, tel: 67296, Morgan Scales, 24 Sth Frederick Street, tel: 60701, and other less well-known auctioneers all send out lists each week to flat-seekers. They ask for references, their prices are relatively dear and you may be charged an induction fee of £5. But they check the flats before they list them so they are all comfortable and in good condition. It all comes fairly expensive but at least you know you're safe with them.

Houses. By dint of looking hard and for a long time you can find a house in the suburbs to share with three or four friends, and it often works out cheaper shared between all of you. Auctioneers are the people, again, to go to here, though there are a few house ads in the *Evening Press.* Landlords are often a little wary of a mixed bunch of communards; you have to look con-vincing. It is a very civilised way to live *if* you have enough space and do not oppress each other, and *if* you all lead much the same kind of lives and have mutual understanding about the way things should be run. Otherwise it is pandemonium, and you will find yourself wanting to run home to Ma.

Au-pairing. If you haven't much money but have evenings free, it may well be an idea to try advertising yourself as a resident baby-sitter. For three or four nights a week staying in to watch the telly and listen for the baby crying, you may be able to get a family's spare room for little or nothing. Make sure it's a family you like, however.

Things to look out for. No matter how eager you are to find a place to rest your suitcase and your weary head, look at your future home with a cold and calculating eye. Watch out for:

1) the **ceiling**: any signs of damp? Is the wallpaper festooning down in ribbons or the plaster about to spatter the carpet? If so the roof needs looking at and you will contract pleurisy if you spend a winter underneath it.

2) **light**: is there enough? There are ways of making a place look lighter but if the place is really funereal you will be too depressed to try any of them.

3) Are there enough **sockets** in each room for fires, beside lamps, radiograms, et cetera? Again there are ways of getting round this problem, but even so it is anguish to choose between a warm silence or music-on-ice or drying your hair in the dark on a lonely and frosty February night.

4) Do the **windows** look snug and reasonably draught-proof?

5) Is there a **ventilator** in the kitchen and bathroom to let smells out? Over-boiling cauliflower can drive a cook out onto the pavement.

6) Does the **geyser** in the bathroom work?

7) What are the **beds** like? If they look like an alpine range and feel like gravestones, no other gracious extra will make up for them. Have a bounce on them first.

8) Is the **landlord's flat** immediately underneath? Or in the same house? What are the **other tenants** like, and are the **walls** the fragile plasterboard kind that you can hear a person yawn through? This is very important.

9) Think about **what you want to do** in the flat. Will you need a desk to work at, and bookshelves? Do you cook a lot and want a fridge and the kind of cooker you like? Are there nice comfy places to sit, and adequate means of heating without running up astronomical electricity bills? Is there enough room to swing a cat —or a flatmate—in?

If the answers are not to your liking, ask the landlord if he can do anything about them. If he can't, work out whether it is worth your while doing something to remedy them. I once found a flat in which the answers to all these questions were wrong, but was so anxious to find somewhere to live that I took it anyway. I ended up moving out again after four days. So be warned.

There are the other questions to work out as well. How near is the flat to your work? Or to a good bus route? Is there room for your car or bike? Are there good shops nearby and preferably one that stays open if you want to buy bread and milk of an evening? Is it near enough to friends or a public phone or a pub in case you get miserably lonely? What about a launderette? Generally it is the very expensive areas that are bad for these: in posh places no one needs a little-shop-around-the-corner because they all have cars.

Your future home might fail in every respect, and yet you still fancy it because of a low rent or because you like a cherry tree in flower outside the back door. But think hard before you hand over a month's rent.

2

LAYMAN LAW

It is sad how many tenants find themselves homeless or in trouble some other way, simply because they do not know their rights. Quite often landlords don't know the law either. So learn your rights and you won't be messed around.

The landlord doesn't have as much on his side as you might imagine. But what he always does have is the law of supply and demand. There are more people needing flats than there are flats and furnished rooms to go round: for this bald reason he can charge a lot, and pick and choose his tenants.

There is no Rent Tribunal in the Republic, although there is a crying need for one. Nor are there anti-discrimination laws to stop you being turned away if you are black, long-haired, have children or are a student. It's not fair, but that's the way it is. Of course it all looks completely different if you happen to be a landlord.

The law on landlord and tenants is so amended and so hopelessly ramified in Ireland that finding out what is legal can take years. Here are some very simple points. For further advice you will have to go to a solicitor or to one of the Free Legal Advice Centres.

You can't be put out overnight. No matter whether your flat is furnished or unfurnished, no matter whether your rent is a week, a month or even six months overdue.

Notices to quit. You can receive a Notice to Quit—usually a piece of typewritten paper asking you to leave your flat or bedsitter by a certain day. This doesn't mean that you can be forcibly thrown out, even when the Notice expires. If your landlord tried to eject you bodily, it would be a breach of the peace. But if you tried to stay, you would probably find yourself liable for 'mesne rates' —usually the equivalent of your rent.

Eviction. To get you out the landlord will have to bring a case against you in the Circuit Courts. This can take as much as a year, or as little as a month to six weeks, if you have no defence. That gives you at least a month's breathing space to look for a new place, or to consult legal aid.

But in any case taking you to court is something the landlord won't particularly want to do, because it is

12

tedious and expensive. And you, on the other hand, will probably not want to stay in the house if it gets to that stage. You will at least have time to consider what you do want.

Leases. Signing a lease is a good idea for your security: the rent cannot be raised until the lease is due to be renewed, unless there is provision in the lease for a rent 'review', in which case it will probably be 'reviewed' upwards. You generally sign the agreement for a year at a time, and if you want to renew it when it expires you re-sign. If the landlord does not offer you a written agreement it would be a good idea to write him a letter confirming terms and keep a copy. The letter would give you strong protection if the landlord should ever come to court, so long as he does not reply contradicting some of the terms. If you are sharing a flat with several others, get them to sign the lease too. If the lease is for longer than a year, the landlord has to sign it as well. In fact he ought to sign even if it is for less than a year, but it is not fatal if it can be shown that he or his solicitors prepared it, since he cannot then deny the fact. You are sometimes asked to pay stamp tax when you are signing a lease. The rate for a rent of over £100 pa is 50p for each £50 of rent. There is no fractional rate, so a yearly rent of £360 should mean £4 stamp duty. You do not have to pay solicitor's fees since the passing of the 1967 Ground Rents Act.

The Landlord. You may be dealing with the landlord's agent, rather than the landlord himself. At any rate find out his name and address and telephone number. Get a carbon of the lease and keep it carefully. Before you sign the lease *read it*. This sounds ridiculously simple, but it nevertheless saves pain later on. For instance, is the use of the garden included? Get that made clear, and any other point you can think of.

Sometimes the agreement will include rates. If the landlord has not mentioned anything about them yet, but they appear in the lease, put a question mark beside that clause and return it to the landlord.

Electricity. Does the landlord say he will pay it? (Unlikely.) If he does, though, write it in on the lease. Leases ought to be very specific. Make sure the dates are filled in for the commencement of the lease, i.e. when you start paying rent. Your length of tenure should also be stated.

Check. Are there any blank spaces left between the lines of the lease? Is your name filled in? You can write it in yourself in the presence of a reputable witness, if not a solicitor. If there are other spaces you don't like the look of, insert question marks and return to the landlord to fill in.

Making Insertions. If you have an insertion to make about electricity or rates, don't worry about the correct legal terms. You are all right so long as the meaning is clear.

Deposits. You are often asked for a month's rent in advance—in some cases two months, or anything up to six months. The landlord keeps it as security against breakages, and it should be entered on the agreement.

Get a receipt for it on the spot. Even if it is only the back of an old envelope, with 'Received from . . . . (your name) the sum of . . . . (the rent) as a deposit for the tenancy of . . . . (address) signed . . . . (the landlord's name). If the landlord is difficult about giving you a receipt then you should try to pay by cheque. If you do not have a bank account yourself, get a friend who has to make out the cheque and refund him, as a cheque marked 'paid' provides the same evidence as an official receipt would. If you don't get a receipt, and at a later date the landlord amazes you by saying you never paid it, there is precious little you can do about it. Too many people have been caught out that way, including me, and it really hurts.

Repairs. The landlord is not liable for repairs unless it says so in the lease. It would be a good idea to note down the defects on the agreement. If there are contents in the flat, an inventory of them all should be made out and checked carefully.

The principle of **buyer beware** applies otherwise; the furnished room or flat is supposed to be fit for human habitation from the start, and you are supposed to have had a good look at everything before you agreed to sign the lease. If major repairs are needed—for instance if the roof guttering gives way and the walls are cascading with damp—then it would be a very unreasonable landlord indeed who would not help. If he does not, and the repairs needed are severe, you can get them done yourself and subtract the cost from the rent.

Trespassing. If the landlord enters your flat uninvited or when you are not there, he is legally a trespasser. However, there is sometimes a clause in the agreement to say he has the right to enter at reasonable times— when the ESB call, for instance, or when the gasman cometh.

Last year there was a long correspondence in the newspapers from a landlord who complained it was terrible what he had to put up with and how his property was abused; his tenants were country girls, he said, who had no standards of cleanliness and left their knickers all over the floor. When someone told him he was not legally entitled to enter the flat, he was deeply amazed.

Squatting. Since the introduction of the Forcible

Entry Bill, squatting is emphatically outlawed. This does not stop people who are driven to it in desperation, but neither does it stop gardaí from forcibly removing them again.

Rent Books. If your rent is payable weekly and you do not have a lease, you should keep a rent-book with your payments entered by the landlord. He should receipt it for you; generally this means leaving the book out on a certain day. (Do not leave the rent out with it if you live in a busy house. Better to leave it with a friendly neighbour to hand over, or give it to him yourself.) If the landlord does not give you a receipt, it probably means he is evading tax, like many landlords in Dublin. This might come in handy, mind you. If he ever turns vicious, you can threaten to ring up the Revenue Commission and declare his income.

Sub-letting. There is usually a clause in the lease preventing sub-letting, and you can in that case be sued for renting out your room or flat to someone else. But if you have to go away for a month or so, and cannot afford to keep it on, it would be a very unreasonable landlord who would not allow you to hand it over to someone reasonably trustworthy, so long as you stand guarantor for the rent. This is why it would be a good idea to let a trusted friend have it; because if the sub-tenant does a vanishing trick, you are liable for their rent.

Notice. If you pay your rent weekly, a week's notice should be enough; and if you pay your rent monthly, a month's. But weekly lettings are a bad idea because it works both ways; you in your turn are subject to a week's notice. Fortnight or even three-weekly tenancies are safer if you do not want a monthly tenancy.

Getting the Deposit Back. It has happened that a

landlord has refused to give a deposit back, or even denied he was ever given one when the lease of a tenant ends. To avoid this, you can use up the value of your deposit for the last month—or two months, however long it is, in lieu of ordinary rent.

Wear and Tear. If your landlord demands compensation, saying that you have left his flat in a deplorable state when you have left, and in all honesty you have not done anything to its condition that living in a place would not naturally do, he has no case against you. This right is known as 'wear and tear' and any landlord should expect it and allow for it.

Here are some specimen problems, answered by a lawyer who specialises in Landlord-Tenant law. But they are about distinct cases; your own will have slightly different features, and may take completely different legal aspects because of them. If you think you have a clear case against your landlord, go to your nearest solicitor. Most solicitors will give advice free to very deserving, watertight cases.

'I pay £4.50 a week for a room with a shared bathroom and kitchen; the landlord says he is putting all our rents up by 50p a week. What can I do?'

'Unless these are rent-controlled premises, or you have a lease, the landlord can put up the rents. If you do not agree to the increase, the alternative available for him is to give you notice. If you stay after a notice to quit has been served, a court may make you pay 'mesne rates' at the new rent level. This is one of the reasons why leases are so important to get hold of.'

'It says in my lease that my husband and I rent our flat on condition that we do not have children. Now I find I am expecting a baby, what shall I do about it?'

'Unless some highflown action can be taken on the grounds that such agreements are unconstitutional or

17

void as against public policy I do not think the tenants are in a very happy position. They accepted the condition; if they break it they will have to leave.'

The geyser in our bathroom has exploded and we cannot get any hot water. It is in a terrible mess, but our landlord will not do anything about it. At least he says he will but that was weeks ago and he has done nothing about it since.'

'The simple answer to this is to get the geyser repaired and deduct the cost of the repairs from the rent. The only difficulty that might arise is that if it is a short-term tenancy, say weekly or monthly, the landlord can always give a week's or month's notice without giving any reason whatsoever to the tenants, but it is probable that the landlord is merely dragging his feet and will not object too much. If the cost is to be deducted from the rent it would probably be better to deduct it over a period rather than take it all out of one payment.'

My room is on the ground-floor and a boy threw a stone at the window last week. There is a hole in one of the panes. Is my landlord responsible for replacing it?'

'That all depends on who is responsible for the repair of what. The tenant may well be liable; if she is, she ought to try to persuade the parent of the boy to pay for it. Strictly speaking the parent is not liable either.'

I share a flat with two other girls and we have a year's lease but now they have upped and left and I cannot afford the rent myself. I want to leave the flat and get a place by myself, but I am scared of having to pay the rest of the year's rent.'

'You would have to pay the rest of the year's rent unless you can persuade the landlord to let you out of it. Alternatively if you find suitable tenants for the landlord he will almost certainly accept them.'

I rent a single bedsitter in my name, but my boyfriend

stays with me a lot of the time. The landlady has found out, and she has served me with a notice to quit. Do we have to go?'

'The landlady is entitled to do this if the letting was of a single bedsitter. Even if the tenant suspects that it is the landlady's outraged moral conscience that is responsible for the notice this is not relevant. She would be equally entitled to serve the notice if it were the tenant's sister who was sharing the premises.'

Organised Help

FLAC. An organisation called the **Free Legal Advice Centre** gives free legal aid to those who cannot afford to go to a solicitor. Most of their work is done with juvenile offenders, teenagers in court, but FLAC workers—most of whom are law students—will help with any legal problem. They are waiting for a room beside the Circuit Courts where you can call in the daytime; meanwhile you can visit them in the evenings at any one of these seven centres :

Ozanam House (St Vincent de Paul), 53 Mountjoy Square, Dublin 1
Open Wednesday nights 7.30–9.30
Director : Dave Maloney

The Dispensary, Ballyfermot
Open Wednesday nights 7.30–9.30
Director : Guy French

20 Molesworth Street (the HQ of the ISPCC), Dublin 2
Open Tuesday nights 7.30–9.30
Director : Brian McGovern

The Basement, Patrick Pearse Tower, Ballymun
Open Thursday nights 7.30–9.30
Director : Barry O'Neill

St Mary's Youth and Community Centre, Monkstown
Avenue, Monkstown
Open Wednesday nights 7.30–9.30
Director : Justin McCarthy

The Boys' School, Rialto, Dublin
Open Wednesday nights 7.30–9.30
Director : George Gill

The Social Centre, St Agnes' Convent, Armagh Road,
Crumlin
Open Friday nights 7.30–9.30
Director : Bill Early

FLAC in Cork
Ozanam House, 2 Tuckey Street, Cork
Open Wednesday nights 8.00–10.30

FLAC in Galway
Ozanam House, St Augustine Street, Galway
Open Tuesday nights 7.30–9.30

The Dublin Flatdwellers' Association. This came into
being two years ago; its aims are to agitate for a Rent
Tribunal in Dublin and to halt rent-increases and evic-
tions. It battles for the maintaining of health regula-
tions and against overcharging on, for instance, ESB
meters. It also wages a long and wearying war against
racketeering flat-letting agencies that profit from the
desperate and unsuspecting home-seekers. The DFA
gives advice to those with landlord problems and will
send a group round to anyone threatened by illegal
eviction by force.

If you would like to bring a problem around to them,
or help in the organisation yourself, they hold meetings

on Thursday nights at :
18 Vernon Street, South Circular Road, Dublin 8
(behind the Meath Hospital)
Secretary: Catherine Collins (ring on Thursdays
between 6.30 pm and 9 pm, tel : 756902)

Alice and Peter Kehoe (Site 29, Donahies, Raheny)
began **Home** in an effort to help young couples whose
rents are too high to enable them to save a deposit to
acquire their own homes. The plight of the young couple
with small childen is desperate : only one in two hundred
landladies will take them, and rents will be at least £40
a month in return. With incomes of £1,500 or over, they
are just too rich to qualify for a local housing loan but
too poor to amass enough to put down on a house. Home
holds meetings to share experiences and to discuss future
means of organising co-operative housing. If you are
young, married, have children and are still too poor to
scrape a deposit on an ordinary £6,000-£7,000 house in the
suburbs, visit Home to pool resources and suggestions.

The Dublin Housing Aid Society.   There comes a time in
every flatdweller's life when they say 'This is no way to
live' and it isn't. Buying houses becomes increasingly
complicated and expensive. John Donaldson runs an
information service for young couples who want to save
for a house; he also runs two half-way houses for desperate families. Consultation hours are Monday, Wednesday and Friday 6 pm–10 pm; Tuesday and Thursday
2.30 pm–6.30 pm.

Address : Dublin Housing Aid Society,
Bewley's Chambers, 19–20 Fleet Street, Dublin 2, tel :
778646.

3

MOVING

Personal memoirs section. I started flat life five years ago with one large suitcase, one medium suitcase and a straw bag containing a map of the world and a bicycle lamp. And it is a constant source of wonderment to me, twelve flats later, that I now own an iron-and-brass bed, a baroque bow-fronted cabinet, a marble-topped toilet stand, two trunks, a tuck-box containing rusting tools, a chair, three mirrors (none of them particularly good for looking at yourself in), a window-box, a paraffin-operated tin-plate percolator, a full complement of bed linen, bolsters, two cushions, a portrait of Charles II with a wormhole, two antique sewing machines, one elderly typewriter with an 'o' that makes bullet holes, flower vases, a white parasol, a poker-and-irons, three alarm clocks, a hat-stand with a hanger population in the hundreds, two tea-chests of books, a dyed thrush in a glass dome, a pewter beer-mug, a guitar with Marty Wilde's capodistra, boxes of ageing letters and photographs, a gas-operated fridge, a china bucket *and* a basket containing a map of the world, a copper gasket and a bicycle lamp. Most of them are rarely where I am. I do not understand it.

I have moved five times in the past three-and-a-half months alone. You would think I had perfected the art. Well I haven't, but I know what I should have done.

Techniques section. If you have too much stuff to cram into a taxi or a friend's car, even for several trips —or if you suddenly don't seem to have any friends any more, you should track down some of the **removal people.** They are advertised in the evening papers, and hire costs upwards of £3 depending on the volume of stuff and the distance it is going. My lot, for instance, was a crippling £8. Get a price estimate from a few before you start.

Go on a **cardboard box** collection to your local grocer several days before you move. Most grocers are affable about handing you over a few, especially if you give them some warning. You can beg wooden boxes from greengrocers, or buy the extra tough kind from friendly publicans for a few bob. Box-suppliers charge a few shillings per box. You can collect them from Shankill's at the Bridge in Shankill, tel: 852676. They make superb shelves afterwards and cost 50p each.

Tea-chests if you want to store books, clothes, etc. can be bought for 5p each from tea merchants like the Irish Tea Brokers at 143 Francis Street. Two jeans-wearing people can carry one chest home by hand between them—but not very far. If you are a student of Trinity College you can get tea-chests from Mrs Crawford of the East Theatre and store them there over the vacation. Most landladies, if you are full- or semi-board in digs, will look after things for you—sometimes for a small fee. A friend with an attic or garage is the next best thing. Places where anyone can store trunks and tea-chests: warehouses like Chris Carroll's, tel: 42197, will estimate a charge for the amount you want to store. They will also collect the chests. Barretts of 44–49 the Coombe, tel: 755865, will charge 15p a week for 60 cubic feet of storage: enough for two tea-chests. Their delivery charge is £1.75. Look up the Golden Pages for other names.

Trunks will cost you upwards of a quid in the Daisy Market behind Capel Street.

Set all the breakables and spillables to one side and

tuck them nicely into a stronger box, individually-wrapped with towels and dishcloths. Then tuck a blanket or a pillow on top of that. It is just about impossible for anyone to survive a move without breaking a favourite cup or spilling a bottle of shoe-dye all over everything. But you can try.

Reconnoitring. Before you embark, make sure you have the right kind of **plugs** and **adapters** for the flat. Older flats usually have two-point round pins; newer ones have the modern three-point flat pins which take 13 amp fuses. Bring along **fuses** too; big fuses for the power load and lesser fuses for smaller ones; lights and sockets. Remember a light bulb or two and blankets, because some leaving tenants are suddenly gripped by flat-moving kleptomania and take everything in sight with them. And most moving is done at weekends when you can't dash out to get new items.

Essentials. All this packing is sorrowful—because no matter how much you loathed your old flat, or how often the lady next door banged on the wall when you switched on the late-night news, you are still leaving a piece of your own lifetime behind—and exhausting. So pack yourself a little **recuperation bag,** containing a kettle, mugs, tea or coffee, a tin of what you fancy and a radio. Everyone's idea of what should go into a recuperation bag is very different. Mine would contain: a radiogram and records, a bedside lamp (because having to get out of bed to switch the light out is my personal hell), beer and a bottle opener, a hot-water bottle, my patchwork bedspread, a bale of briquettes, a copy of some disreputable reading matter and enough cash to take myself away from all this to the late-night cinema. With those few things around me even a lean-to at the back of Heuston Station would seem like home.

Keys. You can get them cut at most branches of Woolworth's, Switzer's in Grafton Street and most hardware shops.

Locked out? Ring 999 and tell the gardai. They will send the fire-brigade who will break in as gently as possible. They don't charge anything.

How not to be locked out. Always leave a **spare key** with a neighbour, or find an ingenious hiding-place for it. The tops of door-pedestals and under the coconut-matting are rather passé and well-known-about these days. You ought to be able to invent somewhere a little more ingenious than that.

Being broken into. It does happen, especially since we have a trusting way of leaving doors open, so be careful about doors and ground-floor windows.

Insurance. This is well worth the bother, and the small amount of outlay. The Insurance Corporation of Ireland Ltd. of 33 Dame Street, tel: 775841, will insure the contents of your flat for £1,000 at a cost of only £3. You are insured from the moment you phone them, if you want to be.

Putting things to rights. Have you got : a screw-driver (small, for electrical work, and bigger for other things), fuses and plugs, insulating tape and flex, hooks, nails and drawing-pins (for obscuring nasty wall-paper with posters), heat (of some kind), music (of some kind), food (of some kind, failing love), Vim or Ajax and some cloths with a scrubbing brush, washing-up liquid, toilet rolls, sheets and blankets, and a 5p or 10p piece for the gas. You will now last out the first few days.

All this sounds very elementary indeed. But anything is better than finding yourself cold, hungry and alone in a strange place where the silence throbs loudly and the dust lies inch-thick and greasy around the broken geyser and you haven't even got a shilling to put on the kettle for tea. Especially at 10 p.m. on a Saturday.

4

STAYING ALIVE FROM A TO Z

PROBABLY the first thing you will find yourself doing is scrubbing your new flat from end to end, scraping year-old jam off the settee and wondering while you stare in horrid fascination at the mattress which of the former tenants had a drink problem. (It is customary in these parts to leave your flat looking as though eight hundred and thirty-nine Nubian slaves were conducting ritual orgies on the lino before they left.) Next you will probably heave furniture around until your personal whims are satisfied and the lady next door has already rung your landlord five times about the noise.

But there are worse problems to be taken care of: here is an A to Z compendium of solutions.

Aggro

This is something you can do without. I think it is a hindrance to happy living to waste time shouting at your neighbours and writing rude letters to your landlord without very good reasons. Introduce yourselves to the people next door, above and underneath you; lend them sugar and twopenny pieces for the telephone. Then you can borrow in return when you are stuck. Being matey with your landlord means he will find it hard to let you down, and vice versa. So you can see there is practical cunning underneath all this sweetness and light. Maybe Patience Strong was on to a good thing all along.

Alarm calls

The GPO operator will ring you for 5p (7p if ringing a coinbox telephone) if you dial 10 and give the time you want to be wakened at. Less expensive is an alarm clock. Clery's counter on the ground floor of their shop in O'Connell Street, Dublin is particularly good for alarms; you don't need a smooth job—one of those tin-hatted screechers of reliable quality can be bought for under £3. Putting it in a large saucepan will amplify the sound, unbearably.

For the almost-unwakeable deep sleepers, a repeater-alarm is the only answer. These will cost something like £3–£5 if truly effective.

If, like me, you sleep so deeply that you are sometimes taken for dead you have my fullest sympathy. A Teas-made is one answer: you can obtain these from Dock-rells, South Great George's Street or from Frank Nugent, Market Arcade, off South Great George's Street, for £5–£8.

For music-lovers there are radio alarms available, such as the Sony Digimatic. These have a dial which you can set at a certain time to turn the radio on at its loudest. They also have huge white figures that flop over instead of a clockface: unignorable. They are expensive new but you can get a second-hand one for £20–£30 in dealers like Hi-Fi Stereo of 108 St. Stephen's Green. Make sure they work first; getting electrical things mended is a real trauma.

Arrests

Okay; so you're a law-abiding citizen. Or maybe you are a law-abiding citizen with a visiting friend who smokes a little pot on Saturday nights and do not fully realise this is breaking the law until the squad-cars drive past. Or maybe you are marching on a demonstration for good reasons and the person beside you thumps a guard with a placard and you find yourself being taken into the station. If you know what *not* to do you could save yourself from panic, perhaps even from prison.

The Citizens for Civil Liberties offer a card with these points listed on them; you can't take it around with you everywhere you go, though, so have a good read now.

If a garda arrests you he must :

1 inform you that you are in fact being arrested and whether your arrest is under a warrant, or otherwise;

2 tell you at the earliest possible moment what offences you are being charged with;

3 give you ample opportunity to see and read the warrant if you are being arrested on the authority of a warrant;

4 inform you of the actual offence if your arrest is on suspicion that you have been guilty of a felony or a breach of the peace and you are being arrested without a warrant;

5 allow you to communicate with or telephone your family or solicitor as soon as possible after you have been charged;

6 make reasonable arrangements for your comfort and convenience;

7 at your request package and seal any property taken from you in your presence (do not sign for anything that does not belong to you);

8 bring you before a court or a peace commissioner at the earliest practicable opportunity;

9 produce an identification card showing that the garda is a duly authorised policeman if he is not on duty.

The police cannot :

1 force you to come to the garda station unless they have arrested you;

2 compel you to answer any questions or to make any statement—including giving your name and address—unless you are obliged to do so by statute : for instance in the case of a road accident where you must by law give your name, address and particulars of motor insurance;

3 hold out any inducement (a deal) or make any promise or threat in order to force you to make a statement;

4 compel you to sign any statement;

5 compel you to take part in an identification parade;

6 compel you to have your fingerprints taken without an order from a district justice or, in Dublin, from the Commissioner or Deputy Commissioner of the Garda Síochána;

7 hold you in custody for longer than a reasonable period without charging you;

8 suggest you plead guilty in court.

You should :

1 remain polite and reasonable;

2 not resist arrest, but try to remember the identity of the policeman and the surrounding circumstances where you feel that you have been unlawfully arrested so that you may be able to pursue a remedy at a later date;

3 not accept police advice as to the solicitor or lawyer whom you should consult;

4 not answer any questions or make any statement until you have seen a solicitor;

5 if you are released contact a solicitor, the Citizens for Civil Liberties or a member of the Free Legal Advice Centre if you are in any doubt about your rights.

In court. If you are charged with an offence do not plead guilty before you have had an opportunity of obtaining legal advice. To enable you to do so, always ask for an adjournment. If you are in custody ask for bail.

The addresses and numbers of your nearest Free Legal Advice Centres are given at the end of chapter 2. The address and number of the Council for Civil Liberties is The Firs, Greystones, County Wicklow, tel: Dublin 874332.

Banks

Current Accounts. I have always found these to be dangerous things, because cheques are still like magic to me and not like real money at all. Starting a bank account is easy, unless you are under 21 in which case you are an 'infant' according to the bank, and your father will have to take responsibility for your account. Which means that when you overdraw on it, it is really your father's overdraft.

Deposit Accounts. These are fine if you simply want a place to lay your dough to rest. Interest on a deposit account is at present only 3 per cent for any amount up to £25,000. You can withdraw your money on request and you don't have to have your parents' signature to start a deposit account if you are under the age of 21. In return you are given a little book to carry in with you when you want to remove your money.

Bank charges are £1 per half-year for up to fifty transactions: if you are likely to be writing more cheques than fifty in six months you will have to pay 50p for every ten extra transactions. There is also a government tax of 1p, payable through the bank when you get your cheque-book, on every cheque you write.

Giro is a way of getting your wages automatically paid into your bank. You simply ask for your money to be giroed in at work. The charges are quite high, though—50p per £50. If you have a deposit account, the giro service costs nothing.

Bank loans are difficult to get unless you are a well-known and loved figure in your bank or a well-established business man or family figure. In which case you won't be reading this book. You can get one, however, if you are studying or want to study. Ask your local branch for details. (You can also get one for a USIT—Union of Students of Ireland Travel—ticket to America in the summer; you can pay when you come back again.)

Bank cards are again very hard to get unless you are an established figure. If you are stuck a long way away from your bank and need money you can go to another branch and they will ring yours for you.

Cashing a cheque can be done at a pub or a shop where you are well known. Since the epic summer of the bank-strike, those hazy days of '70 when people were buying dubious cheques in bundles from little shops in Pearse Street and having the high-living time of their lives, it has become more and more difficult. Short of getting a tin-whistle from Walton's of Parnell Square, I can't think of any other ways of getting cash outside bank hours; I remain open to suggestions, however.

Bank hours are Monday-Friday from 10 am to 3 pm, except on Thursdays when banks stay open till 5 pm. They are shut 12.30–1.30 for lunch. At least putting your money in the post office yields better hours to take it out again.

Bicycles

A cheap, clean, healthy and happy way of travelling to

31

work—or to play, come to that. Dublin used to be—along with Amsterdam and Copenhagen—one of the bicycling capitals of Europe; streams of them combed the throughways of the city morning, noon and night. Now there are 389,338 cars combing the city instead, and the traffic jams would give you thrombosis to look at, never mind drive in. So bicycles are the niftiest as well as the cheapest way of slipping through the mesh. A really smooth Moulton or a Raleigh racing job with choice of five gears is expensive, but you can buy second-hand bikes from the garda bike sale at Kevin Street Barracks, Dublin; these are lost and stolen bikes which are auctioned off twice a year, and the sales are advertised for a week beforehand in the national papers. An old heap goes for a few quid, a really smooth job for £10–£12, and they have motorbikes as well. The only expenditure after you've bought a pushbike is the pump and basket, plus the odd puncture kit and your lamp batteries.

Birds

It isn't just old ladies who like budgies and canaries: anyone living on their own who isn't allowed by the landlord to keep dogs or cats might find a little feathered friend better than nothing. Canaries are traditionally bought in October-November, when they are still rather young. Remember that they are rather neurotic birds, prone to drop dead from heart attacks if a cat so much as looks at them, and that they don't like a lot of noise or travel. They cost £3 upwards, but need comfy cages as well. Belfast's Smithfield market was a beautiful place to buy birds—and white mice; in Dublin there is a bird-market in Bride Street beside St Patrick's from 9–12 on Sunday mornings. However, it is under attack from the ISPCA, so it may not be there much longer. It is a vexed question, this one of keeping birds in cages; you should let them fly around when you are at home and the doors and windows are closed. Canaries, at any rate, would not fancy being let free among the starlings of Donegall Square in Belfast. And I don't suppose if budgies could speak they would ask to be let loose to join their brothers the pigeons on the Dublin GPO roof. But if you do take on a pet you have to think about the chores of looking after it; budgies and canaries don't need to be taken for walks, but they do need to have their cages cleaned once a week, and they like not just doses of bird-seed but the odd bit of cat-nip as well, along with freshly-changed water. They like warmth and sun, and darkness at night and I've noticed that they hate alarm clocks. And you can't go away on holiday and leave them. You can buy all sorts of tame birds, including parakeets, at Uncle George's Pet Shop and Aquarium at 9 Marlboro' Street where there is a Mynah bird called Jacko who can whistle and shout 'gerramoffyer'. The Dublin Pet Stores have birds and also lots of little mirrors and bells for them to play with at 118 Capel Street. Mickey's Pet Shop at 37 Patrick Street and 62 Parnell Street have birds and also breed them: winter is the best time to go and look at them because they nest and moult in the summer.

White mice and hamsters, guinea-pigs and rabbits need a bit more space and cleaning because they can be smelly. They are more companionable but find out what gender they are before you buy them, because they breed like, um, rabbits.

Boredom

This is the curse of lonely bedsitters on Sundays. But you can be bored any time and anywhere. To achieve a really fine degree of boredom try working in a city office from 9–5 and then going home to your lonesome home in Drumcondra or Harold's Cross. But if this is the lifestyle

33

you have decided upon, various remedies are open to you. One that I would recommend is finding out about where you live. When I got my first room in Dublin, I spent days just walking round the city, amazed by the unexpectedness of the docks, the quays, the markets, the Liberties and Smithfield. There was tireless excitement in the crazy maziness of a city where—unlike any place I know in England—you could be asked five bob for an old mattress one minute and the next be staring at the building where Handel first conducted his *Messiah*. It is all being crushed now. 'Progress' to some people means making Dublin into a cheap, plastic imitation of Birmingham: not realising our cultural assets. Soon there will be no more unpredictability, no more architectural ragbags to reveal.

Discovering Dublin can be done in company: the Daonscol (a sort of network of local social clubs, based on Bishop Hedwig's cooperative ideas in nineteenth-century Denmark) plans little meetings and group expeditions to explore the activities of each area. These can be anything from a walking tour organised by Eamonn Mac Thomais to an evening out in a pub where the Swords mummers play and sing. Students can join for 50p, individuals from £1 and families from £1.25. The Dublin Regional Group is based at 27 Grosvenor Road, Rathgar, Dublin 6. The secretary's name is Margaret Saunders: you can write to her for further information.

There are little knots of enthusiasts forming themselves into preservation societies and residents associations all over the county, of course: Swords Progressive Preservation Society is a strong and healthy one, so are those for Blackrock and Castleknock and of course the Ballymun and Ballyfermot organisations. There is a thriving community centre in Drimnagh, bent on showing the world that Drimnagh is the only place to be. They all have different reasons for being. Some, like Howth Preserva-

34

tion Society, aim to keep the beauty of the area intact so that people can stroll through it of a Sunday enjoying the good weather or bad weather without finding themselves in someone's backyard or behind a gasworks. Others, like the Liberties Association, are more social in aim: their targets are better housing where there are gaps and blasted sites, and the rehabilitation and conversion of older buildings into old people's centres, youth clubs and meeting places. All of them are social in the best way: they help people living in an area to get to know each other.

Breakfasts are things that most flatdwellers haven't seen since they left home. But we are always being told how good they are for us: the only good reason I can think of for getting up earlier to make one is that there are extremely few places in central Dublin where you can get a cheap, light snack lunch without queueing for hours. So if you have a breakfast, you will manage through the day with only a couple of sandwiches or an apple and a yoghurt at lunchtime. Here are a few suggestions that don't take long:

Muesli is a Swiss dish that people think of as crank's health-food. You can buy it in packets (Alpen) but it's nicer and tastier to make your own. Soak a bowl of oats in a pudding-bowl overnight (pin-head oatmeal is best but porridge oats are fine) in just enough milk to cover. Add a chopped unpeeled apple, raisin, nuts, dried or fresh apricots or any other fruit you fancy plus a little sugar to taste (brown sticky sugar is nicest). When you get up you can add banana slices, a little lemon juice and—if you have it—a dollop of cream. Wow.

For the culinary imbeciles who have been fed by Ma all their lives, here's how to make the more conventional breakfasts.

Boiled Eggs. Put a pan of water on to boil. When it's

bubbling, put your egg in: don't have the heat up too high or the egg might crack and then you'll have frills of egg-white round the pan edge. A normal egg takes 4 minutes to have a solid white and a runny yolk. Hard-boiled eggs take up to 10 minutes. N.B.—You should never keep your eggs in fridges; it makes them crack, and anyway eggs are little tiny fridges in themselves.

Poached Eggs. Put a little salt in your boiling water (gourmets say you should add a drop of vinegar as well) and break your egg on a saucer; some deft people can somehow manage to get it onto a big spoon and lower it in. Beginners, however, can simply turn the heat down low, slide the egg in from the saucer and spoon it out after 3 minutes.

Scrambled Eggs. People have actually come to blows about how the perfect scrambled eggs should be scrambled. For your début, however, break 2 or more eggs into a small pan and whisk them with a fork (I like to ram the fork into a corm of garlic before using it; this gives the egg a pleasant whiff of garlic without choking it)—add a lump of butter, a pinch of salt and pepper if you like it, plus a drop of milk if you insist—(I think milk spoils the golden eggy taste)—and stir very gently over a quiet flame. Take it off the flame when the scramble looks as though it's on the verge of soggily setting, never when it's actually set because it goes on setting when you are taking it away. Now add another lump of butter. Eat. You can add a pinch of mustard or onion powder or even a few flakes of hard cheese to make it more interesting.

Sausages, Eggs and Bacon. Put a frying pan on the heat and add sausages (*don't* prick them) and bacon first. This is because they take longer, and also because they are full of lovely fat to cook in. When they are nice and brown, turn the heat down a little and gently add the egg—and, if you have it, a halved tomato. If the pan is too hot the egg will glue itself to the bottom and go black round the edges. I don't know how you avoid the yolk breaking; I always break mine. Fried bread in the leftover fat is a delicious extra. N.B.—Don't wash away your bacon fat: keep it if it's reasonably clean, or wipe the frying pan with a piece of newspaper in the time-honoured tradition.

Porridge. Put 1 cup of porridge oats, 1 cup of water and a pinch of salt into a saucepan. Cook it for roughly 5 minutes till it is gurgling like a hot mud-spring. Add sugar and milk and eat. Alternatively add salt, then toss a caber.

Health-fiend's Special. In America people have liquid-isers so this is easy. You can of course buy a liquidiser here, or an electric orange-squeezer which costs less than £5 and is a merry little thing that whizzes around while you hold an orange on its head. But with an egg-whisk it shouldn't take you long to make this by hand. Squeeze 2 oranges and pour the juice into a glass. Whisk 1 raw egg and add it. (Here the novelist Barbara Cartland would add a dollop of life-giving honey). Drink.

Parisian Special. Breakfasts are rightly despised in France where they have a cup of black coffee and a roll instead: usually the roll is a croissant and it is delicious. You can buy imitation croissants at A La Francaise in Wicklow Street; warm a little before eating. They sell partly-baked bread for you to warm up; I wonder why they don't sell partly-baked croissants? See also **Coffee.**

Budgets

Hollow laughter. The publishers asked me to put some-thing about home economy in the book; and since I only know one person who is not actually in debt, and who is rumoured to be living on £5 a week, I asked her what her economies were.

She told me that it was impossible to stick to a budget: the ESB bill will arrive one week and the next you will have to go to the dentist. You may be doing fine until you stroll past a shop window and decide that life will not be worth living unless you buy something inside. Making your own clothes is economy, cooking your own food is economy, walking home instead of getting a taxi is economy, borrowing someone else's paper to read and watching someone else's telly is economical entertainment. But you need time, and you need to think about it all too. It is just about possible, doing all these things, to live in Dublin on £10 per week and manage one drink an evening as well. It is a bit cheaper in the North. But it's boring.

Buses

are the only way to get from one place to another if you have no car or bike in Dublin. And they are doing a grand job, though fares have risen from the 4d I remember from four years back to 4p, a 150 per cent rise in the cost of busing. CIE produce an indispensable little bus time-table, price 3p from all good newsagents; and a very nice little book it is too with a section called 'Places of Interest' which will even tell you how to get to Croke Park for the All-Ireland. I have only one quibble with CIE, who otherwise I think are great (down with cars! ! !) and it is this: there is only one east-west cross-town bus service, the 18, which goes from Sandymount to Bally-fermot, and was started by William Martin Murphy, the *Independent* tycoon, to take his workers to work. Apart from the 18, anyone wishing to get from one suburb to the next will have to go into town and come out again. Bus info tel: 47911. Lost property office, 33 Bachelor's Walk, tel: 46301. See also **Getting away from it all.**

38

Clothes, cheap

If you haven't got the spare cash to whizz round the irresistible clothes in boutiques, you have a choice of two looks available to you: raffish gypsy or off-duty guerrilla. Of course Dunne's Stores, Etam's, Penney's (all in Henry Street) and Cave Boutiques which have branches in Thomas and Fleet Streets can all come up with nice garments for next to nothing.

For the **raffish gypsy** look, you can scour the markets. The Daisy Market (behind Capel Street, next to the fruit-market) and the Iveagh Market in Francis Street have mountains of every type of garment from furred old woollens to whalebone brassières. They also have velvet curtains and the odd piece of brocade that you could sew your own things out of. The market-ladies get their stuff from the Vincent de Paul sales, often held in the Mountjoy Square headquarters on Friday nights: they are advertised in the evening papers under 'Miscellaneous'. One exceptionally good buy: the extra-long sheer black tights you can buy on one of the stalls in the Iveagh Market for 10p. They are open every day except Sundays and Mondays till 3 am and don't like you haggling when you first come, only when they know you. There are periodic Blind sales in the Mansion House, Dawson Street. It takes artistic ingenuity to make a look out of old clothes, but with a sewing machine and a packet of Dylon you can manage it. You can hire sewing machines from Singer's of Grafton Street, or buy one on the HP. Byrne's, at 24 Essex Street is the best place to buy second-hand machines; they will electrify old hand ones for around £6.50 and sell them in full working order from £10 upwards. I find the ancient, ten-ton sewing machine the sturdiest and best.

You can sew **leather** with a heavy oldie machine, too: hides go from 50p from Leather Wholesalers like

Boylan's of 48A Camden Street Lower. Be sure to buy enough hides for what you are making (a leather jerkin, for instance, will probably take three) since hide-colours are hard to match if they didn't all come from the same batch. You use Sellotape instead of pins, and a Stanley knife instead of scissors: begin with something easy like a totebag, and use at least a no. 16 machine needle.

For staple, ordinary materials like gingham, denim, corduroy, Indian madras, calico and crushed velvet, Clery's fabrics department beats all hands down—except for Nicholl's of Wicklow Street which is getting better and better, and usually has a lovely sprinkling of nice summer seersuckers or winter corduroys, depending on the time of year.

If you've never done **dressmaking** before, here's what you need to begin. A pair of large scissors (Woolworth's or, for really good shears, Trimmings on Crampton Quay or Singer's in Grafton Street), a box of dressmaking pins, a full-length mirror for you to look at your results in, and a one-sided razor blade or a Quickunpick to rip out all your mistakes. Be resigned to make failures of your first few attempts; they can always be made into patchwork or dusters or cushion-covers at a later date.

There is a wide variety of pattern books sitting happily in most fabric shops waiting for you to leaf through them; choose one of their extra simple patterns to begin with. When you are getting good at dressmaking you can splash out more on really nice printed cottons and woollen mixtures from Hickey's, Arnott's, Brown Thomas or Switzer's: or the Woollen Mills for tweeds.

Dressmaking without a machine is virtually impossible. But you can make **patchwork** by hand (although it's quicker to sew the little scraps into long strips by machine, then run them all together). Patchwork not only makes pretty cushion covers and labour-of-love bedspreads, it makes nice little waistcoats and skirts as well.

For patchwork you need every last scrap of flowery cottons and plain rags you can dig out from home or salvage from thrown-out clothes. Cut yourself a cardboard shape —a diamond to start with (you need lots and lots, so save cornflakes packets, etc.) about $2'' \times 2''$. Hexagons are more traditional, but they're hell to cut; you almost need a geometrical protractor to do the job, unless your guessing eye is almost perfect. Cut the patchwork scraps so that they extend $\frac{3}{4}'' - \frac{1}{2}''$ beyond the cardboard on all sides; then tack them all onto the cardboard shapes, with the edges folded onto the back. When you have a lovely pile of stitched diamonds, arrange them in a colour pattern— and this is where you have plenty of scope for artistic expression—and hemstitch them fabric-edge to fabric-edge. Then you rip away the tacking stitches so that all the cardboard pieces fall out—and *voilà!*

Little drapery shops are great hunting grounds for material.

The **off-duty guerrilla** look takes less time and imagination to achieve; and here the small surplus clothing-shops are your best friends; Alpha Bargains, Upper Liffey Street and the Clothes Casket in St Mary's Abbey (to the left after Even Steven in Capel Street) are the best. Here you can equip yourself with serviceable jeans for a couple of quid, top them with a white T-shirt you could dye or even tie-dye or a second-hand jersey, even a Guinness jersey. Cheap oilskins and PVC macs are sold for £5–£6, plus plimsolls and boots. Fitzpatrick's of Thomas Street are similarly good for T-shirts and socks, as are many of the gents' clothiers in Camden Street. For more tips on dyeing and tie-dyeing see **Tie-dye.**

For jeans the best shops are O'Connors of Abbey Street and the Jean Machine of Duke Street. (If you live in Belfast you can send away for all those brushed denim elephant flares and loon-pants, desperately trendy, which are advertised in the London Sunday papers and *Melody Maker* and cost £2 upwards by post.)

Coal

is good, cheap, slow heat, but no good when you come home blue or get out of bed frozen and need an instant warm. If you have somewhere to store a winter's worth in October, it will cost you around £5 including delivery. You can order it by telephone and have it delivered from merchants like Heiton Coals, tel: 772931; McHenry Bros., tel: 752311, McLennan, tel: 774592; Sheridan Bros., tel: 771335; or Tedcastles, tel: 717141. (They won't deliver less than a bag at a time.)

Extra big packets of firelighters from hardware shops work out cheaper. Get them wrapped in newspaper before you bring them home; otherwise the smell of paraffin gets itself all over everything else in your shopping basket. Both coal and firelighters have to be stored in a dry place, or you will find yourself doing what I did last winter: plugging in an electric fire to dry out the coal to make it light.

See also **Fires, Making them.**

Coffee

If you drink it in large amounts, or your friends drink yours for you, the cheapest way to buy it is to invest in a giant drum from Woolworth's for £1.90 (about 50p less in the North). It tastes like old dust to a true coffee connoisseur, but costs much less than those tiny little 13p freeze-dried tins in the end. If you like the real McCoy coffee, you will already know about Bewley's Oriental Coffee Houses. Their coffee varies between 45p and 60p a pound and can be bought in beans (they sell grinders, which are the sure-proof way to get really fresh coffee), or, for the non-purists, ground on the spot for you in their branches at Grafton Street, Westmoreland Street, South Great George's Street and Dundrum Shopping Centre. Bewley's sell the Trinidad Express percolators from £2 to nearly £4, from a very tiny size up to what they call an 18-cup: but this means tiny, tiny little continental *demi-tasse* cups. This makes the thick, black, strong-as-the-River Limpopo type coffee that caffeine fanatics like myself cannot live without. You can experiment at mixing their blends if you have a grinder at home: Java and French for instance.

Milder people prefer the Melita plastic funnels; you put filter papers in them, pile the coffee on top and pour on boiling water. With a flame-proof jug underneath, this system has the advantage that you can reheat it for second cups without burning the good taste. You can also get nice little funnels that make 1-cup coffee for your solitary breakfast. You can, as well, re-use the filter paper at least once. Gourmets swear this method makes the most fragrant coffee.

But you can make a perfectly good brew in a jug, just the way you make tea. Pour boiling water into the coffee grounds, putting in one heaped dessertspoon for every cup; stir it a little and leave to draw. Strain it through a sieve—and if you like, add just a squirt of cold water to make the tiny grounds drop to the bottom. Connoisseurs add a small pinch of salt to sharpen the taste. Bewley's have nice Denbyware coffee jugs on sale, a comforting dark blue or brown on the outside and Wedgwood blue on the inside.

Cool, Keeping things

Look under **Food** for some hints on keeping food fresh without a fridge.

Dentists

are expensive, which is exactly the reason why your
mother kept telling you to brush your teeth. On the con-
tinent people sit around after meals picking lumps of food
out of their mouths with tooth-picks; revolting, isn't it?
But rotten teeth are pretty revolting too—one of the
reasons why your best friend never told you, because they
couldn't bear to get close enough. If you have a **blue card**
(in fact, it's a white card) you are allowed free dental
care at the Dental Hospital in 2 Lincoln Place. Ireland
has one of the worst records for national tooth-decay in
the entire world: if you're still holding onto your own
teeth and are without the magic blue card, you will have
to find a good dentist yourself (ask a friend to recommend
you a good one) and pay him for each course of treatment,
but you will probably be able to reclaim some of the outlay from Social Welfare. By the way, it's no good brushing your teeth, they tell me, unless you brush them for at
least three minutes. You can get electric tooth-brushes
from posh chemists. False teeth can be mended on the
spot at Sharkey's of 65 Parnell Street, or 74 Dame Street.

Depression

hits all citydwellers regularly; if you are felled by a fit,
you are being entirely normal. For short-term cures, the
things that work (on me, anyway) are: sleep, playing
doleful records, going to films (but not late-night horror
movies by myself), reading an all-absorbing book, taking
a walk (see **Getting away from it all**), talking to someone.
If you have no one to talk to and are really desperate,
ring up the **Samaritans** at 778833. They are there all day
and night to talk you out of lying down under the nearest
bus, taking a bottle of Codeine or whatever it was you
were about to do. Sympathetic doctors may give you
Valium or other forms of tranquillisers, or send you to a

44

psychiatrist. I have tried both these remedies in vain.

Doctors

are very important to you, not necessarily for saving your
life but for helping you if you have problems or need
someone to talk to. It may not be their job officially; but
it becomes that, probably much to their annoyance, in
practice. So go on changing doctors—don't be afraid to
—until you find one that you really trust and like. Ask a
friend to recommend you one. Students have no problem
here because their college health services operate free of
charge. If your doctor thinks you are fairly poor, he will
probably not charge you much; but specialists can be
very expensive.

Signing on with **Voluntary Health Insurance** is
essential. You may have a scheme at work for group-
payment; even if you earn less than £1,600 p.a. and are
stamping a Social Welfare card—and therefore qualify
for treatment under the Health Acts free—you can be
treated in a semi-private or private hospital room and
choose your own surgeon and physician under the V.H.I.
scheme. Payment rises from £1.20 per annum; you can
write to V.H.I. at 20 Lower Abbey Street, Dublin 1, tel:
49171 or 48751 for particulars. Cork: 70 South Mall,
Cork, tel: 26082. Limerick: 4 Hartstonge Street, Limerick, tel: 45657. Galway branch: Hession Centre, St
Francis Street, Galway, tel: 3715.

Voluntary Health Insurance does not cover:

1 anything you might suffer from up till thirteen weeks
after signing on (in other words you can't think you are
getting appendicitis, say, and rush off to sign up with
V.H.I. before you go to hospital);

2 regular drug treatments and medicines: you can't

claim for them until a year after you have joined the scheme;

3 having babies—unless you've been in V.H.I. for a year and are unlucky enough to need a Caesarian section or have a miscarriage;

4 epidemics, which are declared as such by the Ministry of Health and for which everyone is treated free;

5 less than a day's stay in hospital (except in certain cases which are outlined in the V.H.I. booklet);

6 preventive or convalescent treatment (rest-cures and the like);

7 routine dental treatment (fillings, etc);

8 cost of spectacles, contact-lenses, false teeth, hearing aids, etc;

9 expenses arising from war, invasion, act of foreign enemy (!!!);

10 anything which needs treatment and which you can be compensated for by someone else—as in an accident where you are awarded damages—except at V.H.I's discretion.

It may save you some weeks in bed, by the way, to get an anti-flu injection from your doctor in late summer; or to take regular vitamin C tablets from October onwards. It's true you can get vitamin C in oranges and sunshine, but when there is no sun and now that oranges aren't what they used to be, a course of Multivitamin tablets is worth the bother of taking.

Drink

Where to get it. All alcohol is cheaper from big supermarkets and off licences rather than straight from your local boozer. The cheapest wine is now about 50p (if it's less, it's probably not drinkable) but for that you should manage a good Hungarian wine, if not a grand cru of Chateauneuf du Pape. If I were you I'd be suspicious of wine which says on the label that it is produced in Ireland; it is probably chemically produced—as are many French and Spanish wines—since Dublin is not yet overrun with vineyards. It makes you drunk; that's about all you can say for it. 'Bottled in Ireland' is different of course.

For a good party drink you can buy a fortified (and how!!) cider called Orchard Glow; for making the greatest number of people drunk for the lowest cost it is definitely the winner. Opinions as to the taste vary. You can order it in bulk from Lennox Chemicals at 3 South Leinster Street, tel : 63543.

Brewing your own is less difficult than you'd think, and costs a mere $2\frac{1}{2}$p a pint with not too much hard work. Brewing kits for best ale, lager and stout cost 62p from Rowan's of Westmoreland Street and Capel Street; they make about four gallons and in addition you will need a new plastic bin with a lid, or similar container, to hold the beer, some three yards of plastic tubing (also available from Rowan's), a thermometer—of the big farming variety, not a home-medicine one—and a bottle-collection with screw-tops; washed out vinegar bottles, fizzy lemonade and barley-water bottles, anything like that. Remember to sterilise all bottles thoroughly, because the slightest speck of dirt will cause a disaster. You can also use ordinary beer bottles if you invest in a crown-topper. You can buy wine (red or white) and cider kits from Rowan's for 95p and 50p per two gallon amounts respectively. But it takes two months to make, and needs space, and reasonable warmth as well. Poteen is illegal, and smelly besides; it may be made in garages in Raheny, but it's far too complicated for a Terenure bedsitter.

There are **wine societies** you can join which offer special vintages for members; if you are thinking of becoming a winetaster in a big way try the Dublin Wine Society, 13 Fitzwilliam Square, tel: 65964. Even if you are not a member, you can buy good wines in bulk at very reasonable prices from the Dublin Wine Society or from Wine Enterprises, 2a Brookfield Avenue, Blackrock, tel: 881039.

For the less ambitious, some of the main bedsitterland **off-licences**: Byrne's, 90 Lower Mount Street, Dublin 2, tel: 66194 (they will also deliver for parties, and hire out glasses on receipt of a deposit); Sean O'Neill, 184 South Circular Road, Dublin 8, tel: 751804 (also delivers for parties); Bartley Dunne's, 32 Lower Stephen Street, tel: 753137 (a very good selection including Greek and Chinese wines).

Drugs

The first point to note is that **drugs are illegal** in Ireland, so be warned: if you do take them, you run the risk of being picked up by the Drug Squad. However, drugs are fairly easily available here, and drug-taking is on the increase; I will list the main kinds found in Dublin, so that if someone should press one into your sweaty little hand, you will at least know what it is and what it will do to you.

Hash (or hashish), which is also known under the medical name of cannabis and is nicknamed 'dope', 'shit', 'pot' amongst other things, looks like a lump of solid, very dark tobacco. It has been smuggled into this country, by the way, with almond icing on top in little wedding-cake boxes since it could also resemble fruitcake. It sells from roughly £10 per ounce according to the quality. People can bore each other for hours disputing the various merits of Lebanese hash over Afghani; however, there is not usually much choice in Dublin since what's available depends on who last came back from which part of the Middle East without being caught. It is usually smoked but it can also be put inside cakes, cookies and fudge, and

48

in this way it can be eaten unawares. Opinions vary as to whether it is addictive in the strict sense; most informed opinion would seem to hold that it is not, though a psychological dependence is sometimes built up. The effects of long-term consumption are likewise controversial. But it can be confidently stated that **it does not:** make you insane, lower your morale, turn you into a drug-crazed long-haired morally depraved hippy, nor are any of the other more hysterical charges brought against it true. The report by doctors on the Advisory Committee on Drug Dependence (the Wootton Report, available from Her Majesty's Stationery Office in Belfast or London for 37½p)—states that cannabis is probably no more and perhaps less dangerous than alcohol. **It does :** give you a relaxed, woozy feeling so that you will not feel worried about anything and indeed if anyone suggests you should worry about something, you will laugh your head off. Unlike alcohol it makes you feel very peaceful and inclined to sit around listening to music rather than talk a lot. But it can sometimes have unpleasant effects too, producing anxiety states or hallucination.

Barbiturates are the medical umbrella name for different kinds of sleeping tablets, and they are both addictive and dangerous. Your own mother could be addicted, since some doctors hand them out like Smarties to patients who complain of nervous tension. If you can only get to sleep by cramming a sleeping pill in your mouth, you may find when you try to do without them that you twitch and vomit. They are taken by the nervous when they have to face up to big social occasions they are scared of, or when life is disagreeably tense: but they make them seem clumsy, even a little drunk. Some of the stronger ones are **Nembutal** and **Seconal.** They are specially dangerous when taken after a lot of alcohol; if you are half-doped having taken some, and take some more accidentally, you

49

can easily kill yourself with an overdose. Which is exactly what Jimi Hendrix and Janis Joplin did. Next time you think: I must have a sleeping-pill/tranquilliser, it would make more sense to sit down and work out what horrible problem you are trying to cover up. What is it that you hate so much you can't stand? How can you avoid it, get rid of it rather than become a slave to it by turning to pills?

Amphetamines (Speed) are little pills to buck you up; students doing examinations look for the commoner kinds such as **Dexedrine, Drinamyl** made up as blue tablets or as capsules (green at one end, transparent at the other with little green and white grains inside), **Preludin** or **Methedrine.** High dosages can cause acute excitement, aggression, headaches, all the symptoms of a very high state of tension followed by suicidal depression. In London and New York they are commonly available for a couple of bob from illegal dealers; they are rare here since the Government's Control of Amphetamines Act: as somone said 'Dublin isn't a Speedy city really'. Thank God, no.

Acid (Lysergic Acid Diethylamide), usually now dropped onto pills like the commoner amphetamines rather than on blotting paper or sugar cubes, is quite easy to make and therefore relatively common. It costs anything from 75p to a couple of quid. It is one of the most dangerous drugs if misused, and if you insist on taking it, you ought at least to know what you are letting yourself in for.

People who take acid in alien surroundings amongst strangers are idiotic; people who take it at a big open-air pop festival or in the front row of *A Space Odyssey* are out of their tiny minds, and are not going to enjoy it at all. I can't think of a moral argument to stop you; it's your own comfort you are jeopardising. But if you don't want to jeopardise other people's as well, make sure you ake it at home or in some place where you are at your ease. Ask a very close friend whom you trust completely and from whom no secret is hid to stay with you when you take acid. It acts from half-an-hour to an hour after dropping it, and the effects may last from four to twelve hours, and can recur for a day afterwards and sometimes for very much longer. And it *can* be pleasant.

The friend should not take it, but sit there to talk you out of whatever fears about yourself or the world you may suddenly discover. He will be very bored because you will be very boring while you are tripping. Don't go out by yourself; if by mistake you do, remember there is no reason why anybody else should see you are tripping.

Acid is not addictive in the physical sense; but a psychological craving can develop which is equally serious. It is a disturbing experience because it frees all the thoughts and reactions you usually damp down inside your brain. It leads to hallucinatory states, and these may be pleasant or unpleasant; they may also be dangerous, leading people sometimes to kill themselves. If you have a bad trip, a friend is not enough : you will need **expert medical help**—see **Aid** below (p. 52).

Mescaline is similar in effect to acid except that large quantities produce nausea. It's scarce; when someone offers you it, at a greater price than acid, it probably *is* acid since it is Mexican-Indian and hard to get in New Mexico, let alone in Dublin. In other words, you are probably being diddled.

Heroin. Now for the really strong drugs. Heroin, which comes from opium, is edible in white pill form, or it can be 'fixed' by mixing the white powder in warm water before injecting it with a medical syringe. It is pretty hard to find, costly (at least £6 a grain) and those people I know who claim to get it here say they do so by breaking into chemists' shops. Registered addicts, however, are given it in Britain on the National Health; some tell the doctors they need more than they actually do, and sell half—which is how the tablets get on the market. The immediate effect is usually an instant feeling of great joy, followed by a feeling of painless comfort and happiness with the world. In practice, the addict is anaesthetising himself from the draggy world and its draggy problems; he comes to need more and more to achieve this effect (although addiction usually takes at least two weeks of taking it daily) and with the increasingly larger doses, he is likely to end up breaking the law to get the money to buy it. By this stage, heroin is the only important thing in his life and anything that has nothing to do with getting it, taking it or getting more seems to him not worth noticing. Eating and washing, for instance, seem pointless.

Getting off heroin produces symptoms like asian 'flu: sweating, trembling, intense depression, diarrhoea and crying like a baby. This is because the person who is used to wrapping himself in a nice heroin cocoon of wellbeing can't face the nasty, frightening, brutal world without its help and protection. To get someone off heroin you have somehow to make their life mean something to them, give them something to live for without the drug. This is where your hardest problem lies.

Methadone is a substitute for heroin; it is less strong, cheaper and comes in tablets and ampoules. It is getting commoner all the time.

Cocaine seems to be very uncommon here.

Aid is available for drug-takers who really want help from the Drug Clinic in Jervis Street, tel: 48782. It is open daily from 9.30 am to 5.30 pm and there are special clinics on Tuesdays and Fridays from 2.15 pm to 7 pm and on Wednesdays from 5 pm to 7.30 pm. The Casualty

Department is always open for emergency cases. The Drug Squad of Dublin Castle, tel: 751356, offer a 24-hour service and they say they will give help without asking for names and addresses. Contact any of these if you get stuck on a bad trip. But remember that in order to be given the right antidote, your helpers need to know which drug you have taken: it cannot always be correctly identified from the effects.

If you want to read some books about drugs there are many on the market but they are not by any means equally reliable. A good one is the Pelican *Drugs* by Peter Laurie. Others include *The Drug Scene* by Donald B. Louria and *The Drugtakers* by Jock Young. There is also a booklet on drugs published by the National Council on Alcoholism.

Drunkenness hurts; the trouble is you never realise until next morning when it's too late. The commonest form of drug abuse is alcohol. The **best cure for a hangover** is not as good as prevention, and the best prevention—apart from not drinking—is two aspirins in a tumbler of milk, if you can pour it without sploshing it drunkenly down your nightie or pyjamas. Even a tumbler of water helps, if you have neither milk nor aspirin. If you never managed to make it to the kitchen, however, and you feel terrible when you get up, fresh air they say is the best cure. (I disagree; I think being sick is the best.) Inasmuch as there is a cure, J. J. Graham have one in their pharmacy in Westmoreland Street. It looks like a glass of stout with a good head on it, costs 5p but tastes sweet-and-sour—some maintain it is the revolting taste that is the cure, since you are so happy to stop drinking it. (While in J. J. Grahams, by the way, take a look at the white china letters on the mahogany cases that say 'Erin's Tears'; these are left over from the time when Charles Stewart

Parnell came to buy his favourite toilet water of that name from J. J. Graham). Drunkenness also kills. It is addictive, and you don't need to be told how many addicts there are in the country: there are, at any rate, any number of times more alcohol addicts than drug addicts. Ask a doctor how drink affects you and he will give you a ghastly, lurid description of the ways in which it debilitates the body, ending up by hitting the medula of the brain and causing . . . God, it's too awful even to think of. It is also very expensive, especially since the 'round' system will knock you back a quid or so every time you drink with friends. If you need professional help in fighting, **Alcoholics Anonymous,** tel: 774809 will give you sympathetic help. This will advise on clinics if you want to go in for the 'cure'. There are quite a number of recuperation hostels around, where you can crawl through the mists back to normal life.

Dumping

is illegal, so if you have a lot of stuff to throw away, you can do two things. Firstly you can consult your local dustmen (times of collection vary around the city): ask them if they will be able to take your broken bed-frame or thrown-out armchair or whatever it is away. If they can, you should tip them about 50p; they're doing you a favour. If it is too much for them to take—(a wall you have pulled down for instance, or an old bath) they will tell you how to get it taken away. You can hire a tip from the Corporation; ring their cleansing department (for central Dublin, tel: 779314) and ask for their advice on the matter.

Ecology

sounds like one of these things rich intellectuals in London NW1 invent because they've got nothing else to worry about. In fact, it's a subject which takes in all the resources we take for granted like water and air to breathe: we are fast running out of both because of our disastrous fondness for cramming ourselves all together tightly into the city. We may find ourselves facing enforced water-rationing, for instance, by 1975 if we go on squandering two gallons of fresh water (the average amount) whenever we wash our hands. Here are straightforward ways for flatdwellers to help in the battle against wasting our natural assets:

1 Turn the tap off again when you brush your teeth or wash your face to help conserve our water-supply.

2 Buy your milk in bottles and remember to take them back to the shop. The companies are losing millions on the unreturned bottles; if they turn completely to plastic cartons there will be even more empty cartons littering Ringsend, Sandymount and Dollymount Strands.

3 Shun plastic containers, because they don't rot, they just clot up the sandy beaches. Have you been to Salthill lately?

4 Don't fall for the Americanised disposable-living con. The whole idea behind those throw-away panties, plastic cups, and other gimmicky modern ideas is to make you get tired or fed-up with what you have, chuck it all out and buy new stuff all the time. So that you are always buying, buying, buying—and chucking-out, chucking-out, chucking-out to keep the national economy expanding. Okay, but Ringsend dump is expanding at the same time, just as fast.

5 Don't fall for expensive, seductive packaging. Manufacturers use eye-catching packets to sell their products at a greatly inflated price: cup-hooks for instance are over twice as much in those little five-a-pack containers with clear plastic windows. In a brown paper bag from an ordinary hardware store they are only about 10p per dozen. Aerosols cost more because 65 per cent of what you pay for is the sprayer.

6 Bring your shopping bag out with you and stop assistants from lavishing all those extra paper bags on you: a pile of paper 45″ high is the equivalent of one whole tree. And trees look nicer growing.

7 Don't use those 'biological' soap powders; they contain chemicals which stop the natural breaking-down process in sewers.

All this has probably made you laugh hysterically. Life's too short, you are thinking, to go back to the old ways of thrift and carefulness. The trouble is that there are simply too many people in the world, and people pollute. We can't go on killing riverfuls of fish indefinitely; this world is the only one we've got. We can't throw it away once it's worn out.

And here in Ireland we are in the unusually happy position of having a population that is still relatively small, space to breathe and an industrial record that was still fairly impressive until the River Burrow disaster. The rest of Europe hasn't been nearly so lucky.

If you agree with me that we should hold onto what we've got read *The Consumer's Guide to the Environment* by Jonathan Halliwell, a 40p paperback published by Pan-Ballantine. It will outline all the ways you can help on a domestic level and explain why. Or you can join An Taisce at 116 Lower Baggot Street, Secretary Kevin Fox. They attempt to protect both the countryside and our older buildings; recently they reclaimed Howth Head for a recreation area—to prevent housing estates from running all over it—and are trying to save our beaches by stopping the scheme to fill in Dublin Bay. Their overall aim is to halt the uglification of our island.

Electricity

must be signed on the moment you move into your flat.

Otherwise you might be caught with the bill of the person who occupied your flat before you; you might even find yourself being cut off for not paying it. And then you would have to fork out the lot to get connected again.

Before, or immediately after, moving in go to your nearest ESB office. Fill in a form (a horribly tedious bit this, almost as tedious as paying the bills) on the enquiries desk, and hand over the deposit which is usually £5 for flatdwellers. If you paid a deposit on your previous flat, the deposit is transferable. When you leave you can get it refunded by cashing in your receipt.

The bills arrive every two months; you can be cut off for non-payment after three months, but in practice this time-limit seems to stretch a little. If you are skint you can postpone the unhappy day by giving a few pounds towards the bill. Do this well in time, however, because the ESB computer is irrevocable and once your cut-off card is in, nothing but time will get it out again; it takes a lot of bother to switch yourselves on again.

Your electricity might be entirely on a meter that takes 10p pieces. Landlords are asked to pay the ESB for the meter-hire. This is why the dial is set at above 2p a unit to cover the cost. Some landlords have been known to fiddle with the dials to make a little extra money on them; if your meters are set above $2\frac{1}{2}$p per unit, your landlord is diddling you and you should point this out to him. ESB say they are not the custodians here, and can do nothing about it. So take a look at the meter before you decide to take a flat finally.

It is the landlord's responsibility if a coin meter is broken into.

If you cannot believe your bill, examine it hard. The code number 13 is for the ordinary supply at .84p per unit. Fires are very expensive; a one-bar fire uses two units an hour, so about twenty units in a day. That will be forty units for a two-bar fire. The sum comes to 33p per day, and some £2.31 a week, excluding extra use at weekends, and nine weekends can make this a very nasty amount. So this is where you are forced to economise.

Immersion heaters are the other real killers for expense. They are usually 50p per week, but if you leave them unlagged this loses the heat and can shoot the bill up to £1 a week. So make sure your water heater is well lagged with cotton wadding; if the worst comes to the worst, even a few old blankets strapped tightly around the water cylinder will help.

Lights, irons and radios cost peanuts compared to anything with an element. Even if you use them a lot, they shouldn't cost you much more than £2 per bi-mensual bill. Providing, that is, you do not leave lights on all night and regularly burn right through your ironing board.

ESB insist on safety standards when they connect a supply; they will not allow exposed wires in bathrooms or even light switches; they emphasise that fittings should be earthed and they recommend the new three-point flat-pin plugs with fuses in the plug. The old two-pin plugs abound in more ancient flats; they are often dangerous because it is difficult to get adaptors for them, and people are thus tempted to overload the sockets by combining the wires in the plugs.

ESB says it likes to think that in its own small way it has done a lot to raise the tone of Dublin flats by insisting on high standards of safety and encouraging landlords to renovate their flats. But you would do well to keep a spare supply of fuses and bulbs—and a drawerful of candles for the next ESB strike.

Equipment

If the flat is a furnished letting, your landlord is supposed to supply the basic equipment: a kettle, a tea-pot, a frying-pan, a saucepan or two, a couple of plates, cups, saucers, knives, forks, spoons and a dustbin. There should as well be curtains at the window and blankets on the bed, and if there isn't an open fireplace he should give you adequate electric or gas fires to compensate. With a comfortably equipped flat on a lease, these are listed on an inventory and you should tick them all off with the landlord before you move in, since you'll be responsible for replacing them if they are nowhere to be found when you leave. If they're just not there at all, and the flat has been stripped bare by former tenants, make a list of what you reasonably need for your landlord to supply before you move in.

I've always found that flats are emphatically full of what you don't need: greasy old antimacassars, for instance, and patterned chair covers of the kind that give you delirium tremens to look at, and there's nothing to boil yourself a cup of tea in.

Kitchens need an expensive initial splurge if you want your home comforts. However, it is money well invested: here is the very least you can get away with.

1 a **kettle** (Woolworth's is a good place for kitchen equipment of a rudimentary nature, also Clery's basement. A nice big four-pinter should knock you back around 95p).

2 a solid **frying-pan,** the thicker and deeper the better. It won't just be for fry-ups; where space, money and expertise won't permit you will have to cook a lot of other dishes in that pan as well. The very best you could ever have would be the unglazed, black cast-iron le Creuset (stocked by Brown Thomas). Nonstick ones are expensive and you have to be careful not to scrape their bottoms with a fork or a fish-slice; it ruins their non-stickiness. You can, however, spray a non-stick surface

59

onto a ordinary pan with a spray called Superflon from hardware shops.

3 a **big saucepan,** big enough for boiling spuds and rice, and making yourself warm, wintry soups. Again it will knock you back nearly a quid.

4 a **little saucepan** for your breakfast egg, your boil-in-the-bag frozen kipper or—when you're getting ambitious —real coffee for your supper-parties. Some day.

5 a **very sharp knife.** And if you have to cut up bits of revolting stewing-meat as well as chop onions swiftly, only a really sharp one will do. The French Sabatier knives from Read's of Parliament Street and Broderick Bros. on Wellington Quay cost up to a quid for a large range of sizes, but are well worth the outlay.

6 a **mixing bowl,** for salads and puddings and whatever needs to be mixed. One of those big, white steamed-pudding bowls from Woolworth's, or the yellow-glazed cake bowls with a flat place on one side to balance it while you mix, are best.

7 a **slice** for lifting things out of the frying-pan. Not plastic, nor even plastic-handled; burning plastic is one of the nastier smells of flat-life.

8 a butterfly **tin-opener** (not the jerky kind that lacerate your wrists but not the tin). You can get the butterfly ones for as little as 12½p.

9 a nice big **metal spoon**—not just for lifting eggs out of the saucepan, but also for measuring flour and sugar. For reference: one heaped tablespoon=1 oz flour,

BUT one heaped tablespoon=2 oz sugar (because sugar lies heavy, as they say).

10 a **wooden spoon** to stir with, or two for luck since they're not expensive and it's nice to keep one for sweet tastes and one for savoury.

11 a **breadboard.** Not just for bread, but to save your landlady's table-top when you next make for a pound of onions with your new *Sabatier jaune.*

And after this I would buy myself a sink-tidy, a sieve, a cheese-grater (the Mouli kind from Lambert Brien's of Grafton Street is best because it doesn't spray the pieces and can be held over a saucepan of sauce), an egg-whisk, an asbestos-mat. At this stage, too, I would equip myself with the Penguin *Cooking in a Bedsitter* by Katherine Whitethorn from any paperback bookshop. It is the only cookery book in history written for people who really are coping with one cold tap on the floor below and a gas-ring in the corner, and not much time or money.

You can, of course, manage without all that lot. I did, once upon a time. But I was miserably uncomfortable, spent a bomb on eating out, and in the end I decided the best idea was to learn how to cook.

Learning to cook is merely a matter of poisoning everyone for a few months while you're learning. And the best cooks in history have been men; so masculinity is no excuse for not learning. After you've worked your way through Katherine Whitethorn, you will be highly delighted with yourself and ready to tackle the bigger league—Theodora FitzGibbon's many books, Len Deighton's *Action Cookbook*, beautifully diagrammed for learners; and you will enjoy cooking your way through Monica Sheridan's *My Irish Cook Book* (a Muller paperback) and Kate Engel's *Cooks Know How* (also in the **Lifestyle** series), with a goodly section on party cookery. You may be able to borrow a copy of the excellent Maura Laverty books produced by Odlums and now sadly out of print. And by now there'll be no stopping you; you'll be devouring whole sets of Elizabeth David and munching your way through Mrs Beeton.

For a list of good delicatessens and basic stores, see **Food** below.

Cutlery and delph are also easily bought from Woolworth's and Clery's basement; and you can get special bargains in tea-pots and mugs from any of those strangely fascinating novelty shops down South Great George's Street, and sometimes huge white Carrigaline mugs for 15p or Arklow's Farmel Rose cups at 25p upwards each (these are considered the height of poshness in England where the goodness of Irish pottery is unsung, and you will find them only in the most exclusive Tandoori restaurants) or sub-willow pattern. White sales at department stores like Switzer's where you can buy up absolutely plain white plates and jugs and what-have-you every winter are a good idea as well.

I got almost my entire collection of kitchenware from Mrs Lee of the Iveagh Market in Francis Street. All of it needed a good wash, and I have to say (don't shoot, Mrs Lee) that the prices have gone up something fantastic in the past three years. But it is still far-and-away cheaper and more fun than boring, matching services of the kind that newly-weds' aunties shower upon them.

The junk shops around St Mary's Abbey and at the back of Capel Street are also good for the odd beautiful plate or fancy soup ladle. A Mrs Kelly who has a tiny (nameless) shop there told me last time I went in for a 10p colander that she remembered buying dressers for 2/6d in the old days, delph and all. 'You could be weeks clearing out a cupboard you bought for a couple of shillings,' says she. Ah me, those were definitely the days. However, if you haven't the taste for secondhand kitchenware and haven't the money for new things, the answer is to filch some from home.

Bathrooms need tins of Gumption—(don't use the kitchen scouring-powder on the bath; it scrapes away the enamel rudely)—and either those little suction pads for sticking the soap onto the bath-edge or a plastic shelf for laying across the bath-top to carry your flannels and shampoo, etcetera, and to stop the soap from dissolving in the water. They are fairly expensive; well over thirty bob, sometimes £2, for a lasting one in chrome (which you can undoubtedly live without).

But you can't really live without a toilet-brush. And you may also need an air-freshener to attach to the rim of the toilet-bowl (from any supermarket) or an Airwick, price around 20p. They do actually work, and so does a little crude disinfectant poured down the bowl—and also in the kitchen sink, including the overflow—every now and again.

Bedrooms need sheets and blankets. The cheapest sheets are again from white sales: and then you can get them dyed any colour you like. I've always slept on navy blue sheets, home-dyed (bought from Clery's) and wonder why retailers are unimaginative about colours in general. You can get borders trimmed with elegant Regency green, you can get smothery flocks of sugar-pink flowers, you can get candy-striped Winceyette . . . but for the love of heaven you cannot find plain, bold and bright colours, at cheap prices.

Fitted bottom sheets don't slide up at night or need re-smoothing and it isn't too difficult to fit your own by running elastic around the edges. You can tack corners onto ordinary sheets very rapidly to save yourself from having to leap out of bed to remake it in the middle of the night.

Army surplus blankets are cheapest—around £1 for a grey woollen blanket with a red binding or a white stripe at the top. Functional and warm, they are to be found in drapery departments like Clery's or Heaton Brothers of 42 Thomas Street at sale time. But in the end you may decide that duvets are worth what they cost : from £14 for a single size upwards, plus the cover. You can buy them from J. P. Glass of 30 Wicklow Street, or most big department stores.

Or you can make your own duvet by purloining a good, fat old quilt. Find one in the sales advertised in the 'Miscellaneous' section of the evening papers—and make your own cover out of a pair of sheets, just leaving a slit at one side with tapes for trying it on so that you can easily take it off for the laundry.

For furniture and furnishings, see Chapter 5.

Family Planning

There are two clinics run in the Dublin area, and both will advise anyone on means of contraception; they charge according to what the individual can afford, and have a waiting list of a few weeks. They are: **the Fertility Guidance Clinic**
10 Merrion Square, Dublin 2 (tel : 63676) and
the Family Planning Clinic
15 Mountjoy Square, Dublin 1 (tel : 44133).

Most sympathetic doctors will help you, but for information on the subject of contraception you can send away for an extremely comprehensive book published by the Consumers' Association, enclosing a cheque or a postal order for £1. It is called *Contraceptives—a Which Supplement* and is obtainable from the Consumers' Association, Subscription Department, Caxton Hill, Hertford, U.K.

For a pregnancy test, go to your doctor who will ask for a urine sample to send to a hospital laboratory. It will cost you £2 as well as his consultation fees. You can now buy pregnancy testing kits from chemists; you should ask for them by name and give the manufacturer's as well. The brand name is 'Predicta' and it is made by Organan of Cahill and Company.

If you are pregnant you must make an appointment at one of the maternity hospitals (the Rotunda, the New Coombe or Holles Street) as soon as possible as they have long waiting lists for beds, and need to book you in early. They will arrange for you to attend pre-natal clinics.

Abortions (as I need hardly bother to tell you) is illegal here: and Irish girls who go to England for an abortion cannot get it on the National Health Service. If you are pregnant and need help—either in getting your child adopted, in keeping it, or simply to keep going till the birth, there are many organisations to help you (see **Unmarried Mothers** below). There are also hostels such as the Regina Coeli in North Brunswick Street, run by the Legion of Mary for unmarried mothers.

Fires, making them

I envy the countrydwellers who can twitch a twig here, breathe hotly there—and have an instant inferno. Purists will give you all sorts of theories about how you must stack the briquettes from left to right, wait for lulls in the wind, open the door exactly three inches and hold your breath to make it light.

But basically you buy a box of firelighters and a bundle of little sticks from the tiny-shop-around-the-corner, although neither is indispensable. Rolled and twisted balls of newspaper are as good, if you have the time. You then build a pyramid of coals on top of the lighted firelighters, and the (optional) sticks; or, if you are using briquettes, cross them vaguely like the sticks of a wigwam. The idea is to leave the fire a little air to breathe up from the flame to the fuel.

Then you can hold a piece of newspaper across to make it flare, but I always think that's a piece of flashiness, and that if it's going to draw, it's going to draw.

If your fire isn't drawing well, these are some possible causes:

—the chimney needs sweeping (it ought to be done once a year by experts like the Curry Family whose telephone numbers are 692379, 984493, 971003 or 66308 depending on which Mr Curry it is, or the Rooney family at 43250 on the North side).

—**your fire is on the top floor of the house** (when there isn't a lot of chimney left, you won't have much flue to draw with).

—**your firebricks need replacing.** Firebricks are those blackened lumps of porous rock-like stuff at the back of a fire, and they are supposed to absorb heat and project it outwards. Sometimes they get broken or the former tenant goes off with them. So the only thing you can do is buy a new set from Woolworth's; the back panel is usually 50p and the side-panels are about 37½p the pair.

—**there is no under-draw.** Some fires improve enormously if you take away the grim-looking chunk of iron from the lower section of the grate, revealing a choked ash-filled pit underneath the grate. I cleared mine so that there was a gap of three inches between the grate and the floor; the difference to the fire was instant and dramatic and very heartwarming.

All this must seem very elementary if you've been throwing fires together since childhood. But there are some deprived people who had gurgling radiators instead and missed out on the joy. You may think, too, that fires are horrible messy things that are no good when you come home chilled to the bone. But open fires aren't just for keeping warm (you need something extra for that)—they are for looking into, for drawing people together, for making a focal point, for general homifying.

First Aid

A lot of people haven't the faintest notion of what to do if someone has an epileptic fit, a big electric shock or simply faints at their feet. And it terrifies them out of their tiny wits when it eventually does happen. Of course we should have basic first-aid like the 'kiss of life' drummed into us at school. But most of us haven't—so if you want to find out more you'll have to sign on for a course, such as the six classes (one per week) held by the St John Ambulance Brigade every September at 29 Upper Leeson Street.

You know all about ringing 999 in case of accident or fire. If you are not sure whether you need an ambulance or not—or are so panicky that all judgement has gone—you'll find ambulance men are sympathetic advisers. As are the St John Ambulance Brigade, if you ring them at 65757/8/9. For hospital casualty departments see Help.

Here is some essential information in case of accidents. The only trouble is that you will almost always need another person to ring for the ambulance; also, a lay person can do very little and might unwittingly make things worse. What you can do, and must do in the case of a serious accident, is keep passers-by from standing around the victim, breathing all his air and saying 'oo-er' and 'Janey' instead of doing something handy like ringing 999.

For very bad cuts : when arteries are severed and blood is gushing and the victim is literally in danger of bleeding to death, don't mess around tearing your vest into strips to make a tourniquet. Just clamp your hand very hard on top of the artery, just above the cut. Lean your arm heftily on top. Then you can start looking around for tourniquets, once you've staunched the flow.

For acutely bad electric shocks : if the victim is still stuck to the current, you've got to knock them off it somehow without getting the current yourself. If you know where the mains are you can switch it off; if you don't you will need to insulate yourself somehow. This means either seizing a pair of rubber gloves (but how many people would have those at the ready?) or, if its only a house-current, a bundle of blankets or a piece of wood so that you can knock them off the current. Then you give them the kiss of life.

The kiss of life is also what you give drowning victims; it's incredibly exhausting, because you just have to go on and on and on. It's also very depressing, because quite apart from not knowing whether you've caught the person in time or not, if he has been in the water a long time his mouth will be full of seaweed and God knows what, and you will feel physically sick yourself. You pull the head back to open the throat entrance; with two fingers you clean out the mouth; now you close the nostrils with the first two fingers of one hand, while you fit your mouth on theirs and breathe steadily and deeply in and out. Keep doing it until help arrives.

If someone has taken an overdose, and you're not sure what they've taken, the only safe thing to do is to ring the Poisons Information centre at Jervis Street Hospital, tel : 45588.

Fish (aquarium-type)

You can give yourself company (of a rather unresponsive kind that doesn't answer back) and colour and something to watch, for under a quid with a goldfish tank.

Goldfish bowls should only be temporary homes : a full-blooded goldfish will suffer from shocking claustrophobia in a goldfish bowl, not to speak of that being-watched feeling. Get a rectangular glass-sided or plastic tank that you can stand on a tough bookshelf, or big mantelpiece or even a deep windowsill. You can buy your goldfish from Jebis Aquatics of 26 Richmond Street South or 118 Capel Street. Most pet-shops stock goldfish but they have the best range, including all the tropical varieties as well. They will tell you how to build up a little jungle for your fish to explore, and supply you with the decorative waterweed to make it with. You can also plunder rivers and ponds for the stuff (the Dodder Banks and the little canals of Kildare should make great hunting grounds).

When you are filling and changing the water in the tank, use a plastic bucket with a lip; let the water stand for a few hours because it ought to be the same temperature as the tank-water—fish hate being rudely interrupted with gushes of cold tap-water. Change the stale nasty water once or twice a week (you'll need a little net, or a few jam-jars while you're doing it).

Food can be bought from the Pet Shop again : a pinch of daphnia (dried water-fleas) is what they like best.

Tropical fish are glamorous, but they cost more because they need equipment to aerate and warm the water. Jebis Aquatics will help again here.

Fleas

are no respecters of persons, and Dublin is rife with them anyway. So it doesn't reflect on your personal hygiene if you suddenly find lumpy flea-bites on your arms and legs. But they are tenacious little beasties; hard to crush between your nails, and nearly unkillable otherwise— even if you can see them. So the only cure is to hang all the clothes you think are infested above a scalding hot steamy bath, then dunk yourself in the bath too, washing your hair at the same time. Squirt anti-flea powder all over the bedclothes among the blankets and inside your jersey sleeves and overcoat as well.

If you can catch them, drowning seems to be the only way to murder them. Drop them into a tumbler of cold water, and watch them drown slowly; at least, this is what my Granny tells me you do. I always prefer to let D.D.T. do the job because I can't catch them.

Flies

aren't actually harmful if you keep them away from your food, but they're very annoying. The only remedy is to buy a large can of fly-spray and spray vigorously around all window frames since you can't actually keep them shut in summer without choking. It means your windowsills are littered with tiny corpses, but personally I think they're preferable to those nasty-smelling swinging morgues called fly-papers that people used to use.

Food

Basic Stores. You will have to splash out on an initial outlay when you first move into a new flat. Even if you have no intention of cooking much for yourself—let alone becoming a *cordon bleu*—you cannot comfortably do without :

salt (keep it dry)

pepper (white—and cayenne is nice to have too)

black pepper (if you eat meat)

mustard (you can mix it from powder or buy it in tubes and jars)

oil (corn oil being cheapest—specially if you buy it in plastic gallon-size flagons. Olive oil is the tastiest for salad dressings and paellas; you can buy it in beautiful gallon-size tins from Farm and Dairy Produce in Chatham Street. Alternatively, you can set aside a fat-jar for ordinary frying; start it with some dripping and pour off your extra bacon-fat. Clean it out regularly as it can get filthy pretty fast).

vinegar (cider or wine taste nicer. You can make your own delicious tarragon vinegar by buying a sprig of fresh tarragon from Farm and Dairy Produce and putting it inside the bottle. Simply screw the top back on and leave).

garlic (if you're a garlic-with-everything type like me; you can get garlic salt, if you prefer)

lemon juice (probably less trouble in Jif plastic lemon form, though grated lemon-rind is a shame to miss because it's so good in soups, baking and chicken stews)

sugar (and you can now buy the real, brown unrefined stuff in supermarkets here, not just the brown-coloured granules. But ordinary granulated *siuicre* is still cheapest)

potatoes or rice : long-grain rice, not that pearl-rice which is only for rice-puddings. (You can buy the unpolished brown rice from lovely, lovely Magill's of Johnston's Court)

instant coffee or tea-bags

instant milk-powder, for when you run out of the real stuff

bread (or bread-mix if you like)

six eggs (for all the times when there's nothing else)

margarine, or **butter** if you're feeling rich (you can buy butter off the block in the College Dairy, Stephen Street; it's not cheaper, but it tastes extra nice)

jam, marmalade or **marmite** (you can buy home-made jam and marmalade in a number of places around town including the Victory Restaurant at 6 Castle Market, beside the George's Street Arcade; the Penny Farthing at 23 Exchequer Street; the Cosey Stores in Warrington Lane, beside Lower Mount Street Bridge)

mixed herbs (essential, I reckon, because even if you can only scrape three potatoes together for supper, you can make them taste good with a sprinkle of herbs)

And then come **beef-cubes** and **tomato-ketchup** and

71

flour and **spaghetti** and **soup-mix** and **mouse-trap cheese**
and **onions** and **carrots** and all the other things your
mother seems to have automatically, and you seem automatically not to.

But with that first list of basics, you'll never actually
starve. If you keep it all going with one big shopping ex-
cursion at the weekend (most supermarkets stay open till
9 pm on Friday nights) you should only have to worry
about meat, fresh milk, fresh vegetables and presents-to-
yourself from day to day.

Cheap food. You must be joking. Nowhere else in
Europe, apart from Sweden or France, is food as expensive as it is here—except for butter, milk and some meat.
Fruit in particular is deplorably expensive, often in lousy
condition (look at those neat little packets in the supermarkets carefully) and poor on variety. It's particularly
sad when you consider how much space and soil we have
to grow fruit and vegetables on : far, far better than
Britain—and suitable for quite exotic stuff like arti-
chokes, especially down south. Yet they drag out the
same old sprayed, woolly, tasteless apples : even pears are
a luxury for us. And it's not as though they don't grow
here—because they do. Apples actually grow wild in city
gardens beside the Lower Mount Street docks and gasworks. And yet we buy them, imported from France, at
5–6p each. It makes me weep, because it reflects for me a
terrible national tendency to throw away our rich advantages while we chase the things we haven't the resources
for. A sort of economic death-wish. But I digress.

The Fruit Market in St Michan's Street, Dublin 7 (behind
the Four Courts) is unquestionably the cheapest place to
buy fruit. But this takes organisation. Firstly you need
transport, because crates of oranges are heavy. Secondly
you need enough people to share all the booty around :
or by the time you get to the bottom layer of oranges

they will be green and furry. Go at 7 am having organised your transport and your share-out system and you
will be able to buy oranges at 1p each, tomatoes at a fifth
of the current price (the misshapen ones which taste
perfectly good, go as little as 6 lb for 10p) and in the
height of summer, lovely quantities of strawberries and
raspberries. Rarities like peppers and aubergines are
sadly not much cheaper than they are from good grocers.
The system works out best for large families; for them,
buying spuds by the sackful works out beautifully.

Moore Street is great if you make it late in the day, when
prices drop, and if you push on past the corner stalls by
Henry Street down to the end, comparing prices.

Supermarkets are often good for oranges, apples and
bananas. But don't forget, when you shop in places that
offer Green Shield stamps, that you are in fact buying
the stamps at 1/32 of a penny each, so you earn the
prizes with hard pay. Personally I'd rather have the
money. Dunne's seems best for some things, the others
for the rest. You have to work it out yourself.

Woolworth's are best for eggs, going as low as 20p a
dozen. There are also good dairies that sell eggs in South
Great George's Street and Meath Street.

Chatham Street is as cheap as anywhere for good meat;
market-meat always seems a little dubious to me. Byrne's
has the handsomest assistants. Make friends with your
local butcher and always ask his advice on ways of cooking cheap cuts; there's more to a cow than chops, steaks
and roasts. And if you go at a time when he's not particularly busy to cultivate his friendship assiduously, he'll
be pleased.

Delicatessens have been known to give out cut-price
parcels of slightly ageing cheese or salami ends if they

73

think you lock needy. Ask them around 5 pm of a Saturday afternoon.

Special occasion foods. The best deli's in Dublin are:

—**Magill's** of Johnston's Court where you can get just about anything, from nice big German lentils and Würste to the rarest of Indian spices and Chinese condiments, with some nice cheeses and bread in between.

—**Farm and Dairy Produce** of Chatham Street which are the best for fresh herbs and huge cheeses that tempt you to buy them whole.

—**McCambridge's** of 35 Ranelagh Road, who also have a branch in Shop Street, Galway, sell the nicest paté in town amongst other delicious things.

—**Malloy's** of Sandymount Road, Donnybrook and Blackrock also have exciting foods.

—**Smyth's of the Green** have a fantastic array of different kinds of nuts and dried fruit, also Earl Grey Tea and more lovely cheeses.

—**A la Francaise** of Wicklow Street and **O'Sullivan's** of Dawson Street sell the *bonnes bouches* kind of delicatessen food: delicious, expensive little pots of salad and irresistible cakes.

For home-made cakes try the **Victory Restaurant** of 6 Castle Market again, the **Tea-Time Express** in Duke Street and **Bewley's,** of course, among all the others. Bewley's wholemeal loaf, their pineapple creams and Mary cakes and cherry-buns are surely unparalleled the world over.

If you want to launch out into making your own bread, you can buy raw yeast plus a recipe for barm brack and white yeast bread from the **Irish Yeast Company** in 6

College Street. If you can find Maura Laverty's *Cooking With Yeast*, published in conjunction with Odlum's, it is marvellous for breads of all kinds.

For making your own yoghurt—which is pretty easy—you need to buy a small tub of yoghurt to start your own off. Boil a pint of milk : let it cool, then add a heaped teaspoon of natural yoghurt. Leave it in a warm place overnight, and in the morning you will have your own breed of yoghurt. You use the last lot to add to every new lot and it improves all the time.

Keeping things cool is one of the most boring set-backs of flat-life. Without a fridge, you'll have to look after your food; buying small quantities every day is generally the flatdweller's fate. Because coming home to the sausages you meant to eat five days ago—and didn't— or unearthing a carton of milk that has cheesed is disheartening. Not to say smelly, or even dangerous. But there are things you can do about it.

Milk. You can put a bottle in an earthenware jar, a saucepan or even your own wash-hand basin, filled with water. Wet a cloth and wrap it round the top of the bottle with the ends in the water. Leave the whole lot in a darkened place, and it should last an extra day or two— as it will if you boil it, but boiled milk has a taste of its own, not to everyone's liking. Otherwise mixing your coffee or tea with instant dried milk like Dairy Bawn at least saves you from drinking it black.

Incidentally, if you do have a couple of pints of very sour milk on your hands (about three days gone) you can make your own cottage cheese in time-honoured fashion. Tie up a new white hankie or make a small bag out of what they call butter-muslin. Attach it to your sink tap, or hang it over a bowl having poured the solidifying milk in. Drain it for a day, so that the curds remain in the bag while the whey drips into the bowl. Mash and season the curds with salt and pepper—and, if you want to make a kind of Boursin cheese, garlic and herbs.

Butter lasts pretty well anyway, if the weather isn't too hot. You can buy small pottery or earthenware containers that you stand in a bowl of water, or wrap around with a damp cloth again. Margarine of course doesn't go rancid.

Cheese goes sweaty or hard if you leave it too long. A lump of sugar in the dish will stop it sweating; replace the sugar when it's soggy. Wrapping it in foil or a dampened J-cloth will stop hardening—but if it is hard, you can nevertheless grate it into sauces or make toasted cheese sandwiches with it.

Eggs. If they are very fresh when you buy them, they should last for months. Theodora FitzGibbon (who lived several years beside a volcano in Italy without a fridge and managed fine) says she rubs eggs with $\frac{1}{4}$ lb lard or margarine and a teaspoonful of borax mixed. This simply seals the eggs' surfaces; it's a traditional trick. Be sure to cover every bit of the eggshell. Theodora buys eggs in big quantities in the summer when they're plentiful, cheap and fresh—and they last her well into the winter.

Meat is the dodgiest to keep (especially pork and liver). Take the paper off when you take it out of the shopping-bag; the paper gets smelly first and sticks to the meat. You can always fry sausages and mince—and then reheat them later. But you must be sure to heat them all the way through to boiling point, or you will simply activate rather than kill the nasty organisms in the centre and get a bad case of food poisoning.

You can buy tinned meat; Theodora suggests tinned ham as a luscious stand-by; it can be warmed up and grilled with brown sugar and pineapple chunks or fried in thick slices with redcurrant jelly and a dribble of left-over wine if you should have such a thing.

Or you can marinade meat in oil and vinegar (two ablespoons of oil to four of vinegar or wine) with herbs, alt and pepper to barely cover. It only makes it the more lelicious; pat it dry before cooking, and save the marinade for gravy. You can use the marinade again, up to almost a week afterwards. Or you can salt pork or beef by turning it over and over in the pot with salt and rubbing it in; adding a pinch of saltpetre from the chemist will keep its redness—that's what makes corned beef pink.

Soups and stews keep for 4-5 days if you remember to boil them for ten minutes every day. You can keep mutton stew going almost forever like this; frying and adding more meat and vegetables daily.

Bacon keeps for a week in a cool, dark place in those sealed plastic envelopes they sell it in. You can also keep bacon for some time in plastic airtight containers; but you have to wash the plastic boxes very carefully with boiling water after use. Wash your table-top thoroughly with boiling water after cutting up meat as well.

Fish, like sausages and mince, can be cooked so that it keeps longer. White fish can be poached in half-milk, half-water solution, but it is even better drowned in a sauce made from the milk/water it is boiled in, thickened with a little flour and either cheese or herbs, salt and pepper; then thoroughly heated in a hot oven till the top is browned.

But soused herrings are your best bet; they will keep and keep and are delicious cooked in cider, Guinness or vinegar—or a mixture of these. Cold tea mixed with some vinegar and heated gives an unexpectedly delicate taste.

Smoked fish, like cod or haddock, keep well in a cool, airy place but be careful of flies. Ray and sole actually taste nicer when left for two days.

And of course frozen fish are fine, too, as long as you

remember to fumble about for the *bottom* packet in the shop freezer to get hold of the coldest one, and put a plate underneath it when you get home to stop it from thawing all over your landlady's Tintawn.

Mackerel keeps a day, just about; but it's nicest straight from the sea. And in case you should think fish is only for frying, Bord Iascaigh Mhara have a Cookery Advisory Service (tel: 66444) that keeps a steady flow of good fish recipes circulating the country.

Vegetables. Keep root vegetables (potatoes, carrots, turnips, parsnips, swedes—so called because they are, in fact, roots) cool and dark. The shelf under the sink usually fits this description, or even under the bed. They may sprout a little, but they will be fine for a fortnight at the very least. You can freshen them by soaking them in cold water for a few hours.

Cabbage keeps well—try it boiled with a sprinkling of cinnamon some time; it sounds revolting, but it isn't. Leeks keep if you leave the roots on, trim the tops and stand them on their heads in a jug of cold water. Chicory is a good keeper.

Lettuces droop very fast—and the lasting kinds like cos lettuces are very hard to find. Leave them unwashed in a saucepan with the lid on. Always buy them absolutely fresh.

Fruit is tricky. You're O.K. with apples and oranges, at least for a week. But the only way to keep soft fruit like strawberries and raspberries, even with a fridge, is to wash them, pick them over, pat them dry, spread them on a platter-dish and cover with sprinkled sugar. Chuck out the soggies. Even so they will only keep two days—but if you come back laden from the market, and can't eat the lot at once, it's the only thing to do.

Bread. Apart from keeping a packet of instant bread-mix at hand there's no way you can avoid being left with half a stale loaf every now and again. It's the first occupational hazard of flatdwelling. But if the loaf isn't too stale you can freshen it by holding it in a steaming kettle for half a minute (both sides) or brushing it with milk or water, then popping it into a hot oven for another five or six. It's a good idea for Sundays, Mondays and Bank Holidays when the bakeries aren't baking. If it's even too stale for toast, leave it on the bottom rung of the oven when you're cooking till it's golden: if thin you can keep it in a tin for Melba toast (!) or crush it in a clean cloth with a rolling-pin for breadcrumbs. Bread-bins help.

Fridges

open up all sorts of inviting possibilities to you. With one at your side, you can get away with shopping only twice a week—except for bread and milk. But you have to know how to use them—you can't leave pork chops inside for ten days and then expect them to come out smelling like a rose. And fridges need de-frosting every few weeks; read the instructions on this and have bowls at the ready to avoid flooding. You can save bother if you just turn it off overnight once a week with an empty drip-tray. Next day, pour off the water and switch on again. Watch out for ESB strikes and power-cuts; you could wake to find your kitchen floor awash with the sudden thaw.

It's pointless getting the tiniest size fridge; they hold a pinta and a pork chop and that's all. They tax the electricity bill more; and anyway the next size is usually £39–£40 as compared with a little over £30. Tara Electrics sometimes has sales for shop-soiled fridges in the evenings at its warehouse in 1 Blackhorse Avenue, North Circular Road, Dublin 1. Or you can advertise in the evening papers; a medium-sized one should cost as little as £12–£16 second-hand. Make sure they work, however.

O-So-Cools are small camping-type freezer-boxes that do help a bit, so long as you don't abuse them by putting warm things in and ruining the insulation effect. You can get them from O'Meara Camping Ltd, Sunshine Works, 160a Crumlin Road, Dublin 12, and the smallest size costs about £3.

Thermos-flasks. Lambert Brien's, the utensil shop in Grafton Street (which sells everything from Mouli mills to stone hot water bottles), sell those extra-big thermos flasks that will hold 2 pints of ice-cream, say, for £3.20.

Fuses, and what to do when there's a black-out

When an appliance like an iron or a record-player won't work, the first thing to check is the plug. Unscrew it; if it's the new three-point flatpin kind, it will contain a little 13 amp fuse. Replace it, and try again. If your appliance still won't work, it may need a new element; this happens fairly often with electric kettles—especially if you habitually let them boil dry—and it's expensive. Take a look around your other appliances to see if they're working or not; if nothing works in that particular socket, the main fuse has gone. Unscrew the china top from the fuse in the fuse-box. You can tell if it's broken by looking through the clear bit at the end of the china guard; if the little coloured cap on the end seems to have dropped off, it's bust. Better take it along when you're buying the new one; they now come in so many shapes.

Gas

You will usually get your gas for the cooker with a shilling-in the slot meter, loaned by the Gas Board. If not you will be asked for a £5 deposit when you sign on, or perhaps more. In this case your bills will be quarterly; otherwise the gas-man will come to empty your meter every few weeks, and will leave a receipt plus either some refunded 5p pieces (if you used less than you paid for) or a demand for more (if you used more). It is not unknown for landlords to step in smartly and grab the shillings; this is not illegal because they are responsible for the meters, but the Gas Board consider it unfair. The only thing to do in this case is to try to be there when the gasman calls.

The Gas Company has an excellent spare-part service for its cookers in the basement of its headquarters in D'Olier Street. Grill pans (which previous tenants very often steal when leaving) can be bought for 88p and battery lighters for 96p there.

Gas isn't what it used to be and, alas, you can no longer gas yourself with it because it is now 90 per cent oil and largely non-toxic. But it is still explosive, so if you think you smell a leak, ring the Gas Board's emergency 24-hour maintenance department at 771191 at once.

Many bathrooms have bolshy geysers because the landlord installed them second-hand himself on the cheap. They are inclined to blow up; so if you suspect your own either summon the gas maintenance man at the above number or insist that your landlord does.

Remember to turn everything off when your gas goes out before you add another shilling. If you left the oventap on for instance, and then came to re-light it you could lose your eyebrows—and if gas escaped from the unlit pilot-light, at best you would have a nasty smell. So turn the taps off when the gas runs out before you put another shilling in.

I am convinced myself that gas is no more dangerous than electricity. My favourite cookers have all been cast-iron fifty-year-olds. Some gas cookers run on bottled gas canisters; these need to be refilled roughly twice a year. You can get them from Kosangas at 1 Upper O'Connell

Street (ring 45191 for delivery) or from the Calor Sales
and Service Centre at 12 Camden Street, Dublin 2 (tel
751505).

Getting away from it all

is very necessary if you don't want to collapse from
claustrophobia in the city. Here are Dublin's best parks:

the Phoenix Park—with deer, Fairy Glen, zoo, chukkers
of polo, President, Papal Nuncio and all. The best in the
world, I reckon. People keep trying to build on it; long
may they fail. If you drive out to the other side—down
the Strawberry Beds, or past Dunsinea to Dunsink you
will suddenly find yourself in the real country. Buses 10,
14, 23, 24, 25.

the Botanic Gardens, Glasnevin. Open till 6 pm in the
summer, 4.30 in the winter. Closed weekday lunch-hours.
Buses 13, 19, 34.

St Stephen's Green—ducks and a waterfall, and skin-
heads who train their little boxers to indulge in dog-
fights. Closes at 8.00 pm or later in summer; whenever
the sun goes down, in theory.

Fairview Park—football and grass and sea. Buses 20, 30
44A, 54.

Herbert Park—for grassy peace interrupted by the odd
schoolboy.
Buses 4, 10, 11, 13.
    Or, there are the banks of the Canal between Mount
Street and Portobello Bridge.

For farther out try:

picking mussels at Portmarnock—bus 32
lying in the heather at Howth—buses 31, 38

walking around Lake Poulaphouca—bus 65 to Blessington
seeing Castletown House at the Liffey Weir—bus 67
trying the dodgems at Bray—buses 45, 84, 85, 86
strolling beside the Dodder—bus 14
looking at boats in Dun Laoghaire—buses 7, 8, 45A
46A, 58, 59
making a day trip to Glendalough. The St Kevin's bus
goes from outside the College of Surgeons at
11.30 am in winter on Friday, Saturday and Sunday.
Or why not get even farther away from it all by trying
ballooning, gliding, sailing or caving. Look under **Sports.**

Heating

is distinctly cheap in the form of paraffin stoves. They
cost about £10-£14 from hardware shops like Dockrell's
of South Great George's Street or Brooks Thomas' home
equipment section. You can get your paraffin supply
delivered in 5 gallon quantities from stockists like Peter
Rogers (tel : 41647).

Heat is cleanest and safest but most expensive in the
form of electric fires; you can buy perfectly good ones
from Clery's where a single-bar fire can be had for £1.25.

But never leave your fires where people can stumble
over them easily. A friend of mine once sat on my para-
fin stove whilst deeply and earnestly in conversation, and
only when his trousers were aflame did he realise it wasn't
some kind of seat.

Help!!!!

This is a list of emergency phone numbers :

The Samaritans—tel : 778833 (for anyone with acute depression or suicidal tendencies)

The Drug Clinic, Jervis Street Hospital—tel : 48782 (for
anyone addicted to taking drugs who wants treatment **or**
who is suffering from acute withdrawal symptoms)

Poisons Information Department, Jervis Street—tel 45588 (for anyone who has eaten or taken something suspected as poisonous, or a drug-overdose)

Gas Board Maintenance man—tel : 771191 (a twenty-four hour maintenance service run by the Gas Board in case of leaks)

Taxis that operate all night—66666 (Co-Op); 772222 (Ryans); 61111 (Blue Cabs). In Belfast—33333 (Findacab) In Cork till 2 am 21568, 22317. In Galway—3333

Casualty departments. 45479 (Jervis Street) 694533 (St Vincent's) 305705 (Mater) 752983 (Meath) 772606/776239 (Steeven's)
These five hospitals have the busiest casualty departments and they operate a rota system so that at least one is open at any hour of the day or night. Of course your nearest hospital will usually deal with minor domestic emergencies such as burns, bad cuts or the baby after eating the floor polish.

Hire-Purchase

is the quickest way, short of robbing a bank, for the young and moneyless to acquire a radio, a stereo, a motor-bike, a car, etcetera. But you have to be over 21 years of age, and you have to get your purchase form signed by a house-owner. And when you start to think of it, you probably don't know that many house-owners. At least, not ones you can ask to stand as guarantors. See also under **Radio** and **Television rentals.**

Hiring equipment

is the cheapest thing you can do when you need, for instance, a power drill, a big vacuum-cleaner or a Black and Decker for home-cleaning or repairing. You ring up hiring firms like the Rathmines Supply and Hire Service of 15A Oakley Road for delivery and collection. They advertise in the evening papers.

Insurance

is worth it if you own anything. The Insurance Corporation of Ireland at 33 Dame Street, Dublin 2 will insure your belongings for a charge of as little as £3 per annum. For Insurance Stamps, see **P.A.Y.E. and Social Insurance.**

Jobs, part-time,

temporary or otherwise can be difficult to find in a place where unemployment is high. The choice is not huge. For girls : waitressing is tiring, underpaid and can even be dangerous (I remember being attacked by a drunken customer flailing a two-inch strip of cold steak-fat) but at least it's rarely boring. Try all the posh restaurants and diners-cum-discos in central Dublin. Wages are between £1.50 and £3 per night, more if you're lucky (depending on tips), for eight or even ten hours of physical exhaustion. The good places don't have a high turnover in casual staff, which is the major problem. But doll yourself up in your finery, and go round all these places at about 6 pm of an evening. You can at least leave a phone number in case someone has to go off sick, or leaves.

Evening office cleaning can be a bit boring and lonely at times, but means short hours (usually four a night) and relatively high pay. The agencies advertise for staff in the evening papers.

You can advertise yourself as a baby-sitter. Or if you are really good at cooking or dressmaking, advertise yourself as a party cook to cope with other people's dinner parties, or as a seamstress to sew others' clothes.

You can try writing short stories with sad endings for women's magazines. Sooner or later one will be read.

The hard truth is that lots of them aren't, but if (God knows why) you are looking for what are called "openings in journalism" this is the only way to begin : by writing. Short stories get upwards of £20, feature articles get a bit less.

For boys the opportunities are fewer. Dishwashing jobs can be found in chain restaurants around the centre. You could become a freelance painter-decorator, and advertise yourself in the papers.

You could, I suppose, go mussel-picking and take a basket of fresh mussels around the Dublin pubs. But don't pick them from Sandymount or Sutton; go farther out where they're cleaner.

Busking down cinema queues with a guitar or a tin-whistle is highly lucrative.

Pavement-drawing is enjoyable, and generally wins a few coppers.

Late-night shopping and late-night eating

If you live in a flat or a bed-sitter you probably spend most of your days at work or at lectures, in which case it can be useful to know where you can shop after most shops close. Many supermarkets stay open late on Thursdays and Fridays, usually till 9.30 or 10 p.m. and there are also many of those little shops-around-the-corner in Dublin which regularly stay open till at least 10 pm, selling, but not cheaply, nearly everything you can think of. Besides these, here are a few which remain open even later : Mahon's in Rathmines stays open till 4 am. The Leinster Chalet, also in Rathmines, is another very late shop. And then Jem's in Thomas Court off Thomas Street never seems to shut. There are others and a little painstaking searching may disclose one in your own neighbourhood.

For late-night eating up till about 1 am there is a fair

amount of choice among the more expensive restaurants, and the Coffee Dock of the Intercontinental Hotel is open 23 hours a day. Other places where you can find something to eat really late are Shannon Foods—a caravan on Merrion Road which serves take-away foods 24 hours a day—and the Manhattan at Kelly's Corner, open till at least 4 am.

Launderettes and automatic dry cleaners

can be real necessities for the flat-dweller, who often has very inadequate laundering facilities. Here is a short list of some of those that operate in flat- and bed-sitter land:
Coin-Op Centre, Washeteria, 46 Upper Baggot Street
Automatic Laundry and Dry Cleaners, 6 Terenure Road East
Coin-Op Dry Cleaning, 37 Wexford Street
Bendix Launderette, 3 Wynnefield Road
Red Spot Self Service Laundry, 53 Ranelagh Road and 22 Marino Mart
Washeteria, 110 Lower Dorset Street
Washerette, 453 South Circular Road

Lighting and lamps

Lights in furnished flats or bedsitters are invariably high, central and veiled with salmon-pink plastic shades with holes singed in the sides and the fringe dropping off. You can greatly improve a bleak atmosphere and a harsh glare in your room if (having first turned the light off) you remove the shade and the bulb, and attach a light-adaptor. The kind with two outlets is useful because you can plug a reading lamp or sewing machine (or anything equally low-powered) into the second socket if and when your wall-socket is loaded to capacity. But, of course, you must take account of the risk you run of overloading the light-socket. With a long length of flex in the ceiling light-

bulb socket you can hang your light wherever you like
—beside the fireplace, or over your bed with an on/off
switch attached so that you can turn the light off in bed.
Use a cup-hook in the ceiling for hanging it on but beware of trailing flex. Where you need a lot of light (e.g.
for studying or cooking), a 100-watt bulb is suitable. A
75-watt bulb is for normal use and a 40-watt bulb is
dim, for corridors or very soft intimate light.

Red bulbs, I think, make everyone look like Vincent
Price in a Hammer Film remake of Dante's Inferno.
Blue light-bulbs are good for that underwater look but
will make your features resemble hard-hearted Hanna's.
Pink is all right, but I like yellow best; it is the kindest,
both for you and for your room. But all of these are 65-
watt and not really much good for seeing by.

Bottle lamps are easily made from lamp-converters
which you buy from Woolworths' or Arnott's for well
under 50p. You just jam the adaptor tightly into the neck
of a bottle: a cider flagon or one of those pretty little
bottles of Portuguese *vinho* is best for the job.

Anglepoise lamps for studying need not look like rusting cranes; you can buy luxurious Italian lamps with
adjustable beams from shops like Crow of South
Frederick Street or Prior Interiors of Dawson Street. (For
shades, chapter 5, see pp. 125-6.)

Marriage

Getting married is simple. If you do not belong to a
church (and therefore do not consult your local priest or
vicar about getting married) you simply go to 22 Kildare
Street to ask Mr Downey who is the Registrar for
marriages in Dublin to marry you. You are required to
give a week's notice, to obtain your parents' consent if
you are under 21 and to present your birth certificates
if under 25—and to pay £5.25p for the licence. You also

have to arrive before 3.00 pm in the afternoon, and announce your nuptials in the newspapers which costs £8–£9. This is all that Dublin residents are required to do.

Getting unmarried again is a whole lot harder, if not impossible. It is also very expensive. It seems the wrong way round, somehow.

Marriage Guidance

Both the Catholic Social Welfare Bureau at 35 Harcourt Street (tel: 780866) and the Marriage Counselling Service of the Church of Ireland at 38 Molesworth Street (tel: 62800) run courses for engaged couples, and lend a listening ear to husbands or wives with problems. Ring them for an appointment.

Mice

should be your landlord's responsibility; if you hear a furtive scratch-scratch-scratch at night, and investigation shows small black droppings—generally underneath the sink, around the stove or behind the meter: wherever crumbs and lumps of food are prone to fall—you may be supporting a mouse-colony.

Ringing the Health Department of the Corporation (tel: 776811) will produce an efficient mouser in the form of a Corporation Inspector. Ask for Pests. Rats—brown or black—are much scarier because they are so big; luckily they are pretty scarce now except in central Dublin and areas where there are factories and warehouses.

You can buy pesticides to sprinkle around the populated areas and mouseholes. You can still buy mousetraps too if you really think a trap with a dead mouse in it is any any nicer than a few droppings. I was never brave enough to try these remedies, and I like mice anyway; I left out enough old bread to divert their appetite from my flour-bag or cornflakes instead.

Of course you can always buy a cat.

Music

Records and record-players can be found in sales for what they call 'competitive prices', i.e. a couple of quid knocked off. A dead ordinary, non-elegant but working record-player can be as little as £17. Watch for one with a bass-treble tone knob, as well as volume-control and an on-off knob. It's unusual to find these for under £25 but you occasionally find them in sales for a few quid less because the people who used to buy them are now looking for stereos—or because they happen to be a revolting colour.

You can fit a stereo with an arm attachment to dredge off dust, plus a pair of earphones for £5 so as not to disturb others after midnight. And there are armies of lotions, treated cloths and attachments with which you can adorn them. With the ordinary mono you can only buy a cleaning-cloth and change the needles when your records begin to sound like a trench in World War One, and turn it down when the lady next door thumps the wall. I did know someone (a bass-guitar player) who lined his entire room with collected egg-boxes to muffle the sound. But it took an awful lot of boxes.

One advantage of a mono-player is that it does not monopolise your existence; it stays in the background and as it is very much cheaper you tend to kick it around without worrying. Stereos can take over whole personalities and turn a perfectly normal human being into a complete stereo freak, shuddering whenever someone walks heavily over the floor in case they jolt the needle and refusing to allow anyone else to put a record on. They also kill the art of conversation. Nobody can concentrate on saying anything but 'wow' or 'too much, man' when a bass riff is thundering the membrane of their left eardrum through a woofer and the tweeter is perforating their right.

If you want an explanation of those terms and advice on the model you require, and general helpfulness go to Centresound at 2 Lincoln Place, Harry Moore of Dawson Street, International Sound Corporation of 42 Essex Street or Solar Sound at 19 Rathfarnham Shopping Centre.

Electrical geniuses can buy an amplifer, a deck and speakers separately and piece them together themselves; this is a clever idea because different companies are best for various different parts. You can buy occasional bargain offers in electrical parts from stockists. In fact you could build your own stereo set from scratch but it would probably take you a yearsworth of evening-classes in electronics to gain enough expertise. Peat's of 28 Parnell Street stock cheap components.

If you live in the North, the cheapest available all-in system is Boots' for £28—a sturdy and serviceable little model, even if the speakers are a mere 8″ high.

But this is a subject that needs an encyclopaedia and a dictionary of its own.

Now for something to put on your record-player. The cheap labels are especially good for golden oldies— (Chuck Berry's Greatest Hits, for example)—and some classics on the *Saga* label measure well up to the expensive brands (though perhaps not up to *Oiseau Lyre* or *Deutschegramophongesellschaft*!) Be wary of records that have already been bought and played and brought back again; they are sometimes resold as new. Test them before buying as the fault-quota in records is high.

There are good bargains to be got in second-hand shops like the Gramophone Stores in Johnston's Court for classical records and wild old 78 rpm's. For Rock seconds try Tara Records in Tara Street and Dolphin Discs of 58 Stephen Street. There are quite a few second-hand record shops around; they spring up like the grass but often wither away again.

Jazz enthusiasts get great value if they join the Dublin Jazz Society, which is run by Syd Bailey. Send 30p (in 2½p stamps) to Syd c/o the Dublin Jazz Society, 23 Cadogan Road, Fairview, Dublin 3 for a monthly newsletter giving you details of jazz sessions in and out of Dublin, plus reviews of the latest records. Members get discounts on jazz records at Murray's Record Centres of 23 Ormond Quay Upper, Dublin 7; 3 Mary Street, Dublin 1; 71 George's Street Upper, Dun Laoghaire. Also Discfinder at 147 Lower Baggot Street, Dublin 2 and Liam Breen records at 21 Liffey Street Upper, Dublin 1.

Fred Talbot of 58 Harold's Cross Cottages claims he can get any rare American labels within three weeks if you call on him between 6 pm and 7.30 pm of an evening.

Regular jazz-nights are held in the Embankment, Tallaght, on Sundays; Kelly's of Rogerson's Quay on Mondays; Slattery's of Capel Street on Tuesdays and Wednesdays, and also in the Ormond Hotel, the Pierre Hotel, Dun Laoghaire, the Colamore Hotel in Dalkey and the Leopardstown Inn at Leopardstown.

Cork Jazz Society has regular Monday night sessions at the Munster Hotel.

Classical music. To find out concert venues and times, read 'What's On Next Week' in a Saturday edition of the *Irish Times*. For further information join the Music Association of Ireland at 17 Suffolk Street; for an annual subscription of £1.50p per year, you will get Ian Fox's magazine 'Counterpoint' plus tickets for four or five concerts a year thrown in, and all sorts of other goodies.

Ceilidh. *Ceol*—which you can buy from good newsagents like Eason's—is your best informant for traditional music fixtures.

Treoir which is published by Comhaltas Ceoltoiri Eireann will also contain lots of esoteric information about whens-and-whereabouts. You can buy a copy from the Eblana Bookshop in Grafton Street, from Gill's of O'Connell Street or Walton's Music Shop in North Frederick Street—which incidentally is also the only place in Dublin where you can still find the real honest-to-God tin whistle as distinct from one which is aluminium and plastic. You can also order *Treoir* for 90p (the subscription includes six bi-monthly issues) from Comhaltas Ceoltoiri Eireann at 6 Harcourt Street (tel: 757554).

Moran's Hotel in Abbey Street holds ceilidh nights every Friday. The North Star Hotel in Amiens Street holds them Sunday nights, and The Pipers' Club of Thomas Street, which is a well-nigh-unfindable house opposite a pub called Lynch's just beyond the Public Library, holds Saturday night come-all-ye's where everyone joins in for 10p and where you can learn the uilleann pipes yourself. It's great: no wonder they keep it a dark secret.

Night Classes

You can learn anything from carpentry to yoga in your evenings. The choice is wide as you can see from a recent booklet, *Evening Classes in Dublin* (Irish University Press); and the Department of Education's Interim Report on Adult Education published last year by Government Publications. Most technical schools provide evening classes : you can do pottery in Strand Road, for instance. As well there are independent bodies, Gael-Linn for instance, who give crash-courses in Irish. UCD at Belfield has a huge range to choose from : you could try out early Celtic art or Arabic, for example; at the College of Art you could learn jewellery or how to make stained-glass windows. At health-and-fitness centres you can swim and have sauna baths and keep fit with gym classes.

The Department of Education in Marlborough Street (tel : 717101) will answer enquiries about what's available in the 'tecs and colleges. An Roinn Gaeltachta (tel : 755401) and Conradh na Gaeilge (tel : 757401) will be able to tell you how to improve your Irish. Health Clubs are listed in the Golden Pages.

P.A.Y.E. and Social Insurance

Pay As You Earn is the least painful way of paying your tax; it means exactly what it says; you lose some 20 per cent of your wages, or a little over—depending on what claims you make—automatically. It hurts—but a lot less than having to deliver a couple of hundred pounds in a lump at the government door.

Claims are made for dependent relatives (are you supporting a mother? A wife? Children? Or your Great-Uncle-Joe-twice removed?) and also for insurance policies, mortgages (are you buying a house?) and overdrafts, believe it or not. Also you can claim for certain expenses connected with work : businessmen, for instance, do not pay tax on their expense accounts. But you will be given the details about that at your work-place.

Starting work. Unless it is your first job, you will be asked for a P45 form; this you should have been given by your last employer.

If you have never had a full-time job before, and therefore do not possess a P45, your employer will make out an Emergency Card (known in the lingo as a P13 and as miserable as it sounds too, because emergency tax is the stiffest rate) and he should also send a P46 to the tax office so that you will be given a new index number as soon as possible.

Tax refunds, if you are due any, will be given to you after the beginning of the new financial year (which begins 6 April) when your employer has handed you your Certificate of Tax-Free Allowances for the new year. (This is known in the vernacular as your tax-free cert; keep it in a very safe place, and make sure your employer has his copy.) You hand your employer your old certificate—and he sends it on to the tax office in Hammond Buildings. Bob is not your Uncle, but in due course you should receive a nice tidy sum by post. Refunds are given if your certificate (a P6CL) needs amending: if you married, joined V.H.I. or had a baby, say, you must go to Hammond Buildings to fill in a P11 and then wait 4 weeks. You are asked to give the tear-off section of your new tax-free cert to your boss or his accountant again.

Insurance stamps are paid for you automatically if you are a manual worker, irrespective of how much you earn. When you start work you go down to the Department of Social Welfare (An Roinn Leasa Shóisialaigh); Beresford Place, Dublin 1 (tel: 46501) for women, and 50 Lower Gardiner Place, Dublin 1 (tel: 46501 as well) for men. They will issue you with a small blue card, with your name and insurance number filled in. Keep it on your person in a safe place; hospitals, police and other people wanting a means of identifying you tend to ask you for it. Copy the number down in a safe place too.

Non-compulsory Insurance Stamps. If you earn less than £1,600 per annum you are entitled to free hospital care in public wards and are entitled to medical benefits. If you earn more than £1,600 p.a. you do not have to pay insurance stamps: if you do you will enjoy certain privileges and reduced fees if you should have to go to hospital. It's advisable to insure with Voluntary Health as well, however. (See **Doctors.**)

Pensions. Even if you pay no insurance stamps at all, and God spares you till the age of 70, you will enjoy a pittance known as the Non-Contributory Pension. However, if you intend staying alive that long, I would consider taking out a life insurance policy if I were you : it will help your spouse or your children even if you don't.

Working Wives lose out. You probably pay about £1 a week extra in tax for the conjugal joys of being married, but your husband is given an extra tax-free allowance for both of you.

Drawing the Dole. For dole pay you need 26 stamps on your insurance card for the *previous* year that you were contributing them. When you left your job they should have handed you a card with all your stamps neatly stuck in rows. This is your proof.

You are not given dole if the Employment Exchange is not satisfied that you cannot yet find other work suitable for your talents.

How much is the dole? £3.75 per week for any man or woman over the age of 18; £3.12½ if you are a married woman dependent on your husband's wages. Your first two children entitle you to an extra 77½p per week, and after that the rate is 52½p per child. So it would be pretty hard to live on the dole without extra benefit.

Marriage benefits and maternity benefits. Apply to the Department of Social Welfare, Aras Mac Dhiarmada, Dublin 1, tel: 46811, for enquiries. Marriage benefit is between £3 and £10; you need a full three years of insurance stamps to claim and 48 for the last contributory year to get the lot. Ah well, it might buy you an electric Teasmade.

Unmarried mothers are entitled to the same benefits as married mothers: a lump sum of £4 for confinement (you apply to the Department of Social Welfare not later than three months after you have had the baby) and a weekly allowance of £3.87½ for six weeks before and six weeks after having the baby. Unmarried mothers may be eligible for other benefits: enquire at your Social Welfare Officer's counter in O'Connell Bridge House. (See later on, **Unmarried mothers.**)

Post Offices

can be anything in Dublin from the bullet-riddled pillars of O'Connell Street to the tiniest little grocer's shop with a grill in the corner that shuts half-day of a Wednesday. The second kind will often take advertisement-cards in the window. Saving through a post offic account gives better rates of interest than a Bank Deposit account—which is a mere 3 per cent on lodgements. Also, post offices have better opening hours than banks for withdrawals.

Postal Services. The main GPO in O'Connell Street is open from 8 am–11 pm. The Andrew Street branch stays open until 6.30 pm but all other branches shut at 6 pm.

And in case you don't already know, a letter sent anywhere in Ireland or the United Kingdom costs 4p, a postcard costs 2½p. A letter to Europe costs 6p and to America 12p. Air-mail letters are buyable too (the green form which you fold over and stick down) for 7p.

For telegrams, dial 115 if you are ringing from a private phone, 10 for the operator if you are ringing from a coin-box.

From Cork you dial 10 for the operator, whether from a coinbox or a private line; unless you are ringing from a private line with a number that does *not* begin 021–6 or 021–7.

From Galway you ring 10.

From Belfast you ring 100.

There are three deliveries of post a day in the city centre, two a day in the suburbs and none at all at weekends except for telegrams and special deliveries.

Puppies and kittens

Pets are very tempting. Most landlords do not allow them, and they are right. A puppy or a kitten can make a cold, lonely room into a home; but they need space. And a dog or a cat need even more space—and dogs need a lot of walking to boot. Like budgies, geraniums and landlords, they respond only to loving care. You meet too many neurotic, misbehaving dogs who sob in the night and piddle all over the floor simply because their novelty value wore off after three days and now their owners brush the hairs off their jumpers, reluctantly spoon out more Kennomeat into an encrusted, filthy bowl and go out socialising without them.

If you have a decent-sized kitchen, a bit of corridor or a balcony, even a largish bathroom where you can put an ashpan for the cat, it will probably know how to look after itself. A dog will need a run at morning, noon and night; it will also be prone to fits of melancholy if you leave it on its own too long.

But if you are adamant about wanting a furry companion, buy yourself a good paperback on training and pet-care and go down to the Dog and Cat Home on Grand Canal Street where you can save a mongrel or a kitten from the death sentence. Make sure a puppy is vaccinated and, above all, that it does not have distemper.

Radios

become difficult to live without. Transistor radios now begin around £8.95p but the very smallest ones tend to have bad reception, depending on what area you live in.

For better reception and a wider choice of stations you

will do better with a £25-plus job. McHugh Himself of 39 Talbot Street sell these on hire purchase for a deposit of £2.50 followed by 50p weekly instalments—as will most record-player and radio shops. But you have to be over 21 and get the signature of a houseowner (generally one of your parents, someone where you work or even your landlord if you are on genial terms with him) in order to get credit.

Records and record-players : see Music.

Saving and Credit Unions

I have to break the unhappy news to you that saving is no longer worthwhile. In these spiralling decimalised days money depreciates so fast that if you put £100 in a bank you will have to add £2 to it every year to keep it worth the same amount in buying power. Tough, eh? It would be better—if you are saving for something specific like a house—to use a Credit Union.

Quite a few firms have Credit Union groups within their staffs, and so do some housing estates. You become a member of your Credit Union by filling in an application card, paying a membership fee and agreeing to purchase at least one £1 share. You can buy the shares one by one or in instalments if you like.

They are insured, so that if you die your nearest and dearest gets double the amount you had saved when you died. Even if you had borrowed an amount from the Union, the debt is cancelled for you and your family is still compensated.

You can withdraw your shares whenever you like.

You can get a loan for whatever 'in the best judgement of the Credit Committee promises to be of benefit to the borrower' and this is taken to mean a house, a deposit on a flat, a washing machine or a car, school or uni-

99

versity fees, bailing your drunken old Dad out of court again, hospital fees; your holiday, even.

The great point about all this is that the Credit Union League of Ireland is run by bonded treasurers committed to a vow of confidence who work voluntarily to run it as a non-profit organisation. It is a democratic organisation because it eliminates the high rates of interest you pay on other kinds of financial loans, and it stands by you in case you get smit by a hurricane.

The Credit Union League of Ireland at 9 Appian Way, Dublin 6 (tel: 680731) will give you the address of your nearest branch. Cork: Ballyphehane C.U. is in Friar's Walk, Lower Cork (tel: 24442); Blackpool C.U. is at 1 Assumption Road, Cork (tel: 51757). Galway: St Anthony's C.U. is at Mill Street, Galway (tel: 59541); St Columba's C.U. is at 66 Plunkett Avenue, Galway (tel: 5825).

Scabies

is a kind of burrowing parasite between your fingers and toes as well as in the groin. It isn't necessarily a sexual disease; it comes simply from overcrowding and you can get it wherever people are living in squashed conditions; an epidemic of it swept Ireland last year. Remedy: scrub yourself in a very hot bath from head to toe before applying Benzyl Benzoate all over; two stints of this should rid you of the infuriating scratching. The cure for crabs (nasty little lice that live in pubic hair and which also result in unbearable itching) is identical; sometimes shaving is advised as well.

Seating

Seating is most sociable in your flat when it is soft and low. Many people nowadays solve their seating problems by shoving their bedframes in a convenient cupboard and lounging on their mattresses. It makes for a relaxed and comfy atmosphere; the only drawback is that you can't hide your dirty laundry and old newspapers under the bed this way. You can get extra mattresses for lounging on in auction-rooms like Slowey's or Skelly's on the Quays, or in junk shops around the back of Moore Street. And you can buy and cover bolsters for armrests as well: patch them up tightly before you begin with proper patches, however, because escaping feathers drive you crazy.

Clery's, Nicholl's or Central Upholstery of 23 Parnell Street make good hunting grounds for cheap upholstery-covers. You can try corduroy, needlecord, cheap crushed velvet, dyed calico, mattress-ticking, felt—even hessian from Goodbody's. And look out for remnants of beautiful Sanderson fabrics in shops such as Prior Interiors or Brown Thomas; sometimes fragments of Liberty's prints or pieces left over from a huge order of William Morris hand-printed materials are sold off cheap. The hand-woven Donegal tweed blankets—should you be given one for a birthday present—also make beautiful bedcovers.

Covering a sofa or an armchair means equipping yourself with a box of pins and a big pair of cutting shears. Get a friend to come and help you if possible. You cut the shapes out on the surfaces of the chair or sofa, leaving a good fat allowance of two or three inches. Pin the pieces to the chair as you go. Then fold edges under and over-sew rapidly with tough linen thread. It's not the professional way, but it's the quickest.

You can buy yourself a flexible 'worm' for lolling on from Crow's of Lower Baggot Street—they are beautiful to look at, and mould to your shape when you lounge across them. But they are also expensive. You can make your own by sewing a tough cotton 'tube' and filling it with foam-rubber granules (available in huge sacks from

Vita-Cortex of John F. Kennedy Drive, Naas Road or from Kinsale Road, Cork). Cover the stuffed tube yourself with corduroy. Foam-rubber granules are also good for filling those huge luscious cushions about 4 feet square, usually covered with Indian material. Ordinary foam rubber (for sitting on) is available from O'Leary's, 82 Queen Street, Dublin 7. And you can buy Indian bedspreads from the Indian Shop, South Anne Street.

Smells

Smells are the bane of bedsitter existence. Where you have to live, sleep, cook, eat and work in a confined space with a kitchen or a kitchenette that has no adequate ventilation and bathrooms and bins that are shared and dustbins that constantly overflow in the hallway with rotting vegetables sprinkled around and down the hallway, you will smell and your environment will stink.

In the kitchen. Pour disinfectant down the overflow and the pipes regularly. If you suspect something is stuck in the pipe underneath, buy caustic soda and use according to the instructions on the packet. Be very careful about not letting your food go off, and wash out your sink tidy and your little plastic food-boxes regularly with scalding water. Open the nearest window when you're cooking and if necessary leave the door open too. Some say that a crust of stale bread in a pot of boiling cabbage or other vegetable makes a lot of difference. Theodora Fitzgibbon says keeping the lid on and being sure not to overboil will produce only the most fragrant and mouth-watering smells.

It is, of course, illegal not to have some form of ventilation in a kitchen or a bathroom; the absence of thorough health inspection, however, means that a vast proportion of Dublin flats are breaking the law.

Sports

Here are the phone numbers of various sporting associations who will be able to tell you how to join the nearest amateur game if you fancy flexing a muscle.

Ballooning is pure joy, and neither dangerous nor expensive. The Secretary of the Irish Balloonatics is David Synott (tel: 41497) and if the weather proves clement he will arrange for you to make a brief ascent above Kill in Kildare in Tar Baby or Yellow Peril, the Society's hot-air balloons. Usually £1 per flight.

Canoeing is for those who don't mind getting wet. Bill Harrow (tel: 378635 or 809971) will tell you how to join Wild Water, Seapoint or Leixlip Kayak Club. Membership costs £1 per year.

Caving is for the hardy, but once hooked you are never off it, although most cavers will admit the best part is when you're on the surface again, tucking into a hot stew. You will need to borrow a wet-suit—or send away for a cheap stick-it-together-yourself kit, although you can get away with three jumpers, long coms and a boiler-suit the first few times. Ring Eamonn Devoy (tel: 776115) or write to him at 135 Cork Street, Dublin 8.

Camogie. Ring Mrs Purcell at 973180 for amateur fixtures and to see what chance you may have to join a practice team.

Boxing. There are 35 affiliated clubs in the Dublin area alone. Frank Bannon (tel: 312909) will tell you where yours is.

Fencing. For a touch of Douglas Fairbanks-type skill with a rapier try the Irish Amateur Fencing Association (tel: 885081) or taking lessons with Sally Duffy (tel:

693720) who gives lessons to beginners on Tuesday evenings at Salle d'Armes, St John's Road, Sandymount.

G.A.A. You have a choice of 183 Hurling and Gaelic clubs in the Dublin area alone. Ring Jim King at 44734 for information.

Gliding. Contact the Dublin Gliding Club at Flat 15, Glendale Court, Adelaide Street, Dún Laoghaire; a day's try-out flight will cost 50p at Baldonnell airport.

Horse-riding generally costs 75p an hour, £1 an hour for instruction as well. Pony treks are often arranged around the south Dublin mountains. Look up your nearest school in the Golden Pages.

Judo. Get in touch with the Dublin Judo Club, 32 Parkgate Street, Dublin 8 (tel: 775782) to enrol for classes.

Skiing. For dry-skiing instruction to teach you the basics before you head for the snows, contact the Ski Club of Ireland at Knockrabo, Mount Anville Road, Goatstown (tel: 693985) or the Irish Ski School at Santry Stadium (tel: 754483 for enquiries).

Sailing. Donald Archibald teaches sailing from the West Pier of Dún Laoghaire for 60p per hour, lifejackets included (tel: 978415). Or you can join the Glenans Sailing Centre in Baltimore, Cork for two weeks of holiday cum instruction-course for £38 (tel: Baltimore 54).

Swimming. I have it on medical authority that the sea is safe to swim in from Bull Island to Skerries and from Sandymount to Killiney. I have swum in the Grand Canal without dying from typhoid-fever, but then I'm not fussy. I wouldn't advise anyone to plunge into the Liffey— below Islandbridge at any rate. There are networks of canals that are beautiful if a little weedy to swim in around Kildare: near Robertstown in particular. Public baths are: the Tara Street Baths (Markievicz Baths) in Townsend Street which are open only half-day on Sundays, the Willie Pearse Pool in Windmill Street, Dublin 12 (again open only half-day on Sundays), the Clontarf swiming baths with open sea bathing from May to September, the Blackrock Baths, the Northside Swimming Pool and the Dún Laoghaire Baths. Only the Tara Street Baths and the Willie Pearse Pool remain open the whole year. The others open from the beginning of June till the end of September.

Tea

Tea—in case your mother never drummed it into you—is made like this: boil the water, rinse the pot out twice while it's boiling, put in as many teaspoonfuls of tea as there are people to drink it plus one for the pot, then pour on the boiling water. Give it two ritualistic stirs with the spoon, and leave it for a few minutes to draw.

People argue all night about whether or not one should put milk in the cup before the tea or vice versa. I don't know because I never drink it; I think it tastes like washing-up water anyway. But I know from being told that Bewley's is great for tea; that it stocks the exceptionally nice Denbyware tea-pots that are brown outside and china-blue inside from £1.06 upwards, and that it has rare china blends like Lapsang Souchong and Jasmin-Scented Pouchong (the kind with flower petals floating around on the surface); Smyth's of the Green stock Earl Grey tea; and the India Tea Centre of Suffolk Street has a fine range of Indian teas which may be tried out first in the restaurant.

Telephones

are a revolutionary new invention for promoting a spirit of friendly togetherness in the community. It is a shame we have not yet acquired such instruments here—only thrombosis-causing instruments that force you to bang them and smash them in a desperate attempt to get the right person at the other end. By way of compensation, we have the jolliest switchboard operators in the world; which is just as well since we have to overwork them so much.

Getting a telephone installed is an operation of extreme delicacy requiring the patience of a Mandarin. It's not like America where you ring up and ask for a phone and they ask you what colour and would you like the contessa model, and the whole thing's over inside a week. Here you need £45 deposit and at least a year to loiter suspiciously around the city in your spare time, searching high and low for public telephones that work. They take 2p pieces; or rather they don't just take them—they rob them. There are rows of good ones at the side entrance of O'Connell Street GPO, within the Andrew Street GPO, beside the Anne Street GPO and at all other district branches. Hotels, pubs and big department stores also have them: get to a pub where you can pour yourself a stiff drink before you try.

If your flat is already wired for a telephone you should be slightly better off as all they have to do is connect it. Pester the authorities until they do so.

Telephone services

Time (the speaking clock) 1191
Weather forecast 1199
Operator 10 (100 in the North)
Directory enquiries 190
Emergency—fire, police, ambulance 999
Trunk calls 10 (the North, 100)
Person-to-person calls 10 (for an extra charge of 10p)
ADC calls (where the operator rings back to tell you the

cost of the call) 10 again. (There is an extra charge of 5p)

Direct call to London: 031
Direct call to Belfast: 084
Direct call to Cork: 021
Direct call to Galway: 091
Direct call to Limerick: 061

Other STD numbers and charges are listed on the green pages in the front part of the telephone directory. You can buy your own private or replacement copy from Hammond Buildings in Upper O'Connell Street. From Cork or Galway of course the Dublin prefix is 01. From Belfast the Dublin prefix is 0001. And I'm sorry to say the application situation is every bit as despairing in the North, where Donegall Place GPO say they have year-long waiting lists as well.

Television rentals

are reasonably cheap, especially if you are sharing your telly between several flatmates or co-tenants. The lowest rental I know of is for a one-channel 17" (you measure TVs diagonally across the screen) at 40p per week from Telerents of 40 Mary Street. They can sell you a five channel aerial for the unlikely price of £96 and will come round to advise you on reception and tuning if you ring them at Dublin 4000.

Telerentals charge from 52p per week; 64p for a five station Bush including Harlech and BBC2. But again if you haven't got a VHF aerial (one of those four-legged steel cactuses that occasionally sit on Blackrock or Monkstown roofs—or you don't live in an area with piped telly: usually the housing estate areas like Ballymun, Finglas, Ballyfermot or Drimnagh—you've had it. You can, however, rent a VHF aerial—as well as the telly—with RTV rentals for around £5 per month (tel: 64901) and if you want to avoid the bother of getting your licence from the

Post Office you can get an all-in deal with Slot Television (tel: 342122). This can mean, however, the God-awful trauma of running out of 10p pieces in the middle of your favourite TV programmes. *Aghhhh*!!!!!

Tie-and-dye

is easier than you think. To pattern an ordinary unbleached cotton T-shirt, button-down vest or silk scarf you will need: a tin of powdered dye (from Woolworth's or some hardware shops), a large tablespoonful of salt, some kind of stick to stir with and a very large pan. Dye can be bought in liquid form, too, and is, perhaps, marginally easier to use like this. The little bottles go further than the tins of powder.

Washing-machine dyeing is easiest, and you can use cold-dye in the bath (but read the instructions with care). In the ordinary way, however, you need a good supply of hot water and you must follow the instructions religiously. Otherwise you will get dappled clothes and possibly splotchy arms as well. Even pumice stone won't take dye off your fingers; you have to wait till it wears off. And never bung your dyed article in with the rest of your wash or you'll be sorry.

For tie-and-dye the procedure is modified as follows: you tweak little peaks of the material where you want lighter markings before you put the article into the dye. Bind the peaks firmly around with string and when the article is completely dry, cut off the bits of string and iron it. Applying Paintex intensifies colour into a pattern.

Batik is more ambitious. It is an ancient Javanese method of printing with wax: you can make cushion-covers, wall-hangings and beautiful shirts and dresses this way. You need: a small pan, an assortment of small brushes, household candles and an assortment of dyes plus brown paper and an iron.

Put the candles in the pan and melt them. With the melted wax you can paint patterns on the material to your liking. Let the wax dry. Now dye the material, dry it and iron the wrong side of the material onto the brown paper to soak up the wax. Dye it again with another colour and you will have your pattern in two shades. Eason's have a good stock of paperbacks and hardbacks about batik, tie-and-dye, candle-making and other crafts. If you would like to try candle-making or batik you might be interested in buying wax by the half-ton (which is the cheapest way, of course). It can be bought wholesale from Shell B.P.

Turf

The real kind may be ordered from McHenry Bros. of Blackpitts (tel: 752311) who deliver it at £8.5 per ton. They deliver up to 5 tons.

Unmarried mothers

can obtain sympathetic help and a home with a family until after the birth of their babies, by contacting ALLY. Miss Helen Campbell is the Secretary and you can ring her at 43742 in the mornings. Ask for her or the President of ALLY, Father Fergal O'Connor at the St Saviour's Dominican Priory in Dominick Street at all other hours: tel: 43652 or 44245. The unmarried mother can then go to the Social Welfare Officer in O'Connell Street to apply for benefits: these are exactly the same as those for married mothers.

The Church of Ireland Social Service at 39 Molesworth Street, Dublin 2, tel: 62800, also help mothers-to-be to find accommodation and help. They do not try to persuade girls to have their babies adopted against their wills.

Venereal diseases

Clinics for sufferers of VD are held in Sir Patrick Dun's Hospital (tel: 66942), Dr Steeven's Hospital (tel: 776239) and the Mater Hospital (tel: 301935). Ring and ask one of the clinics for an appointment if you suspect you have the symptoms: soreness, a burning sensation when you urinate, and in men some secretion of pus: women will sometimes notice an increased vaginal discharge. In syphilis there may or may not be a noticeable wet or crusted sore called a chancre.

It's a difficult thing to diagnose by yourself; many do not notice it at all until it's too late. Both gonorrhea and syphilis are deadly diseases currently enjoying mini-epidemics in Dublin on the quiet since so few people are taught how to recognise the symptoms and signs. It is too often left uncured or only partially cured—and one quarter of syphilis victims eventually die, crippled by the disease. It is also hereditary, so it is passed down to your children unless it is very thoroughly treated, and in time. Gonorrhea—though less deadly—can cause sterility and insanity. So even though your symptoms may be far less serious check with the clinic.

Voting

Once a year a voting registration form will be dropped in your letter-box. Fill it and return; this will mean you feature on the voting list and will receive a voting card in the case of elections and referenda. You can check in your local GPO if you haven't yet had a form or a voting-card; they have all the registered names on the voting list and you can check against them or file an application. It takes weeks; do it a month or so before Voting Day. They will tell you your nearest polling booth.

Windowbox gardening

You too can go back to the Garden of Eden. With a bit of practice anyone can grow herbs and even tomatoes, as well as cacti and geraniums in a window-box. And with no sill at all to speak of you can have a saucer garden on your kitchen window ledge and bottle gardens around your window shelves and on your mantelpiece. And certain plants—like the well-nigh indestructible rubber plant —will grow in a steamy lightless bathroom with practically no watering at all.

Containers. You can use just about anything you like from a chamber pot to a collander. If you have a stretch of yard or balcony—no matter how small, and a wall— you can go in for potted bay trees, rambling roses, trellised honeysuckle and Yeats' poems. You might even manage a spot of honey—but I wouldn't advise it, since traffic noises seem to make bees angry.

Window-boxes can be simply made with five pieces of old wood and a box of nails. They ought to be at least 6″ deep for the plants' roots to have room to spread, and 7″ across. And coat the inside with rot-proofing from your gardening shop because a filled box can weigh over six stones and if it fell apart or rolled off the sill onto someone's head, you'd be up for manslaughter. So try to fix a metal or a wire strap round it to the window-frame if you can. Otherwise you can buy huge hooks and eyes from ironmongers; you fix one ring at either side of the window-frame and then you jam the hooks solidly into the ends of the box. If your window-frames are metal and open outwards you could borrow a hammer-drill and fix extra-stout metal brackets to support the box, or you could cradle it in doughty metal chains affixed to metal rings in the brick at either side if all else fails. Paint the outside a smasheroo colour—and paint the windowsill surround with whitewash too if you want to really brighten your view.

Other containers. Any big china bowl will look good, particularly soup tureens, while old sinks and halved beer barrels are very effective too—but these take more space. It is difficult to get the old earthenware plantpots these days, alas. But you can make hanging baskets out of anything from a metal sieve to one of those pressure cooker vegetable baskets. And you can buy pottery ones, very pretty hanging over your window frame, for £1 upwards; they are stocked by Market Ireland in Grafton Street and also by the Barrenhill Gallery in Baily near Howth.

Filling them. Because you are cramping a plant into a tight unnatural space, you may have to help it get extra drainage and nourishment. Whatever container you use, there should be a hole of some kind in the bottom. Then you should spread a layer of broken crocks-rubble, pebbles, sea-shells, broken china or bits of smashed old plant-pot—at the bottom. If you have no draining system at all because you are using a china pot or something you cannot punch holes in, put two handfulls of charcoal in after the broken crocks. Now cover with a layer of rotting vegetation or peat moss to act as a juicy sponge for the plant. Your container should be roughly a third of the depth full at this stage.

Have your box in the finished position now as you won't be able to shift it around much. Buy—from a good gardening shop like Rowan's of Westmoreland Street and Capel Street, Drummond's of St Stephen's Green, Caulfield's of 17 Dame Street or Hackett's of 15 Parliament Street—a bag of plant soil to suit what you want to grow. The assistants will advise you; they stock several different kinds for different uses. 'Plant Pack' is the normal variety; it should knock you back around 25p.

Bulbs for your window box. Keep your plants low-growing if your windowsill is high-up and windy. Try keeping something in bloom from early spring to late summer like this:

Plant winter aconite in separate plant-pots in September-October. Move them out to place in the box when they are showing their shoots and there is the odd sliver of February sun. Treat all your other bulbs like this, keeping them in a dark cupboard or under the stairs until they show signs of healthy sprouting. The separate pots make it easy to shift them in and out of the box.

As well as aconite, snowdrops and crocuses are some of the earliest flowering bulbs. Plant them in September/October to bloom in February/March.

September, too, is the month to plant scilla, grape hyacinths and Glory of the Snows. A little later you can plant your daffodils and narcissi (and there are endless varieties of dwarf daffodils, very suitable for high-up shallow window-boxes). All these will bloom in March and April; bring them out of the dark when they are sprouting. If the first aconites and snowdrops have died you can remove their pots and restock with daffs.

December is still not too late to plant some bulbs—the full-sized hyacinths in particular. Try the smaller sturdier irises, and anemones too. They will bloom in April and go on into May if you are lucky.

For summer. Growing from seed will be tricky for you. Far better to stroll into the gardening shop and see what ready-grown plantlings await you. Salvia, phlox, Sweet William, pansies—you will not lack choice.

Herbs are easy to care for : most thyme, sage, marjoram, chives, mint and lavender will thrive, and basil and fennel can also be managed. Incidentally, garlic and nasturtiums grow wild as weed all over this island and both are delicious in cooking—nasturtiums in salads.

In autumn you will have little choice; scotch bluebells are unusual and pretty.

Easy-care indoor plants hardly need watering; some even prefer to be left alone most of the time. No one can go far wrong with geraniums (the flatdwellers' friend, with lots of colours to choose from), maidenhair ferns, tradescantia, variegated ivy—and of course rubber plants and cacti : the modern-day aspidistras.

There are plants that like to be almost totally ignored, such as crassula, Christmas cacti, African violets, gloxinia and a type of geranium. Some—like the brittle sedums, echeverias and sempervivums—like coolness and a little light.

What might have gone wrong. Plants are as bolshy-minded as humans : no one can properly say what will make one plant decide to thrive and another one drop dead. But check for these :

1 are you overwatering them? It's only too easy : stick your finger into the soil and only water if it's bone-dry. Otherwise it would be safer to put the water in the saucer rather than the soil.

2 Maybe your plant is getting too big for its pot. Move it to a larger size.

3 Try a shot of diluted plantfeed like Biotex : spray it in a milk-bottle fitted with a plastic rose, and dilute according to instructions.

4 Is your sill too draughty, or facing north? Pick only the hardiest plants.

5 People tell you to give plants dissolved disprin, or to talk to them aloud in an encouraging tone of voice. W-e-l-l; you could try—if all else fails. For a basically sturdy plant, hospitalisation in the bathroom sometimes does the trick.

Bottle-gardens are easily made in big glass jars, stoppered at the top so that evaporated water drops on the earth again and you practically never have to water them. Capel Street sweetshops—or other sweetshops, come to that—very often sell off their sweet-jars quite cheaply and these make ideal containers.

Ask for very tiny, slow-growing plants in the shops or they will shoot up and crowd each other out of the jar. Let a tiny bit of air in somehow (round the edge of a cork, or by not screwing the lid on too tightly) as otherwise the condensation will be so heated that you will see rivers of plants' breath running down the side but not the plants themselves.

There are tiny dwarf shrublets and Alpine rhododendrons; also tiny willows to make little Japanese and rockery gardens.

A variety of ferns will do well; choose the tiniest of maidenhair ferns and small variegated-leaved ivies like Glacier, Harold and little diamonds. You can also grow small orange-plants and lemon-plants from the pips, as you can in saucers (see section on Saucers later on). But your gardening shop will have advice; and you can trade a few cuttings from a friend's smaller plants.

Saucers or plastic yoghurt-pots with holes poked in the bottom and two tablespoons of scrounged earth will grow the following evergreens in next-to-no-space.

Carrot-tops: just slice off the fat end of a carrot and stand it in water in a saucer near the light. Add a little to the water every day. It spurts very fast, with delicate greenery; you can try the same with parsnip, turnips and other root vegetables. Potatoes (small ones) can be sat on the mouth of a milk bottle containing water; they are slower to sprout.

Watercress: take a piece of flannel, or the kind of sponge they wet stamps with in the post office. Water-soaked blotting paper also works; you simply scatter the seeds across the top, and lovely sandwiches it makes, too.

Apples, pears, plums, peaches, oranges : plant the pips in tiny pots and water when the earth looks dry. After they reach a height of 3–4″ you should move them to a window-box, and then a garden.

Peas and beans: wrap blackeyed beans (from Magill's) or haricot beans in strips of blotting paper which should then be spiralled around them and placed at the bottom of a jam-jar. Water.

None of these grows infallibly. You can do everything for a plant short of breaking a bottle of champagne over its bows, and yet it may go black and flop dead all the same. No one really knows what makes them decide to live or die : you can only guess. But I know a Chinese lady who grows bean-shoots on her sill.

Hanging gardens are lovely, lovely things. Suspend whatever your basket is—open wirework from the gardening-shop or pottery from the souvenir shop, a sink-tidy or whatever—with strong cords from a hook in the window frame. Line it with sphagnum moss from a good florist's or one of the gardeners' shops. You can add an interlining of perforated plastic to retain the moisture as well. Ask for a peaty-based soil to fill the rest of the inside; give it a liquid fertiliser shot-in-the-roots every couple of weeks. Or you can put your plants in the basket with their pots still around them; pack them in tightly with the moss.

Try geraniums, fuschias, ferns, pendulous begonias and small ivies. Ask your shop what trailing plants they have; ask for creepers, which look nice twining up the cords.

Complete the Garden of Eden with a bird table : even half a coconut shell hung by a string from your window frame will do—or a few dangling bacon-rinds : but a board firmly anchored to your sill with hefty bricks is best; the end-piece of an orange-box, nice and light, makes a good table. Leave crusts and bits of left-over cakes : in preference, things they will have some trouble making off with fast. Add a tin-dish of water for a bath, and maybe a little mirror.

For reading and expert help, try *House Plants* by John Compton, published by Hamlyn; *Windowbox Gardening* by Zenia Field, a Pan paperback, and *Windowbox And Tub Gardening* by Kenneth Lemmon which is a Corgi Mini-Book. All are well worth the 15–30p they cost. *Making Things Grow* by Thalassa Cruso, published by Michael Joseph at £2.50 is excellent. So too is *House Plants* by Thomas Rochford, published by Roy Hart at 12½p.

5

FROM TAT TO HABITAT

How far can you go?

Your electricity is connected, your light bulbs are lit and you are happily tossing half a pound of pork sausages into a frying-pan with the record-player blaring when suddenly the thought blazes through your brain cells : 'This place looks hideous.'

Landlords, if they bother, tie themselves into knots trying to achieve a neutral effect : wallpaper to delight an elderly bachelor civil-servant and a dashing young advertising man. They also get things in heavy colours so that a place won't get dirty-looking, and they are great frequenters of carpet sales where they buy pieces of Botanical Garden in lurid tropical colours that knock you flat before you dare to walk on them, let alone wear them down.

I far prefer the kind of landlord that never does his places up, and consequently doesn't mind what you do to yours (within reason) either. Anyway, before you do anything at all, ask your landlord how much he will allow you to transform. Can you paint the walls, ceiling? If they are so wet and crumbly that the paper is dropping off and plaster rains on your head like hailstones, he should look to his guttering and help you with the cost of papering and paint. If the curtains give you migraine to look at and are torn, he might possibly allow you the cost of new ones if they are mutually pleasing. Remember, he probably will be glad if you increase the value of his property—so long as you are in mutual harmonising taste about it, and you aren't clamouring for Deadly Nightshade or Tangerine everywhere.

How far you can go

If the answer is no, no, NO and he flatly forbids you even to remove a lampshade, here are some temporary prettifications: haunt the Iveagh Market (in Francis Street) and the Daisy Market (behind Capel Street) and comb the piles of clothes—politely—for velours to drape the three-piece suite with. Those old-fashioned heavy deep-fringed velvety table-cloths are best.

An Indian bedspread from the Indian Shop in South Anne Street will drape nicely over a divan or a bed and can even be tacked onto the wall with drawing pins or dress-making pins to conceal eye-blithering floral designs on a wall-paper.

Curtains

The St Vincent de Paul sales in Mountjoy Square can be good for pairs of huge velvet curtains, or heavy velours again. Heaps of old upholstering look a bit daunting at first; but you acquire an eye for it. I once got to the stage where I could stare a six-foot mountain of dirty, decaying fabric plain in the face and subtract everything I might be going to be interested in within 30 seconds flat without incurring odium. But you need training, and that means practice.

Hanging them. Hang your curtains with brass-rings from junk-shops, or with little round gold rings (you get them in packets from Woolworth's or Dockrell's) sewn on to the curtains and looped over a brass bar or a piece of cane, bought by the foot from hardware shops again. Cup hooks at either end will support the bar.

You can always dye the curtains you've already got. Dyeing is a question of reading the instructions on the packet carefully, remembering to put the salt in and forcing yourself to do the tedious job of stirring all the time. If you want to go fancy, try **Tie-and-Dye** (see chapter 4, p. 108) or even appliqué butterflies from Weinrib's Trimmings on Aston' Quay.

Curtaining material leaves you with oceans of choice. Clery's of O'Connell Street and Nicholl's of Exchequer Street are the best value for basic materials like corduroy, velveteen, crushed velvet and gingham. Odd but fetching curtains could be made out of pyjama-stripe material (dyed, if you like) or even mattress-ticking. Calico makes lovely ones : you can paint designs onto them with fabric paint, or tye-die them—even Batik them.

Blinds

You have to get these made to order and cost varies according to size. A good furnishing-fabric shop like Nicholl's will look after this problem.

Walls

Buy posters from Eason's, and scrounge what you can from theatres or art-galleries; haunt junk shops for prints and pictures and if you have clothes that are decorative, hang them along the wall in full view of the public. A friend of mine did this with all his shirts: he said he preferred risking them getting dirty to looking at his wall.

For hanging things up. Light things only need dressmaking pins, and the marks they make are negligible. Mapping-pins from a good stationers like Hely's of Dame Street, Browne and Nolan's of Dawson Street and Combridge's in Grafton Street, are pretty little things that don't crater the wall, too. The worst thing you could possibly use to hang something is Sellotape; it rips your poster/print and it strips the wall too. For heavier things you will need tacks and a hammer.

Floors

can only be disguised—if your landlady won't let you do anything with her precious carpet—by more carpets. Arnott's of Henry Street have a magnificent carpet department in their basement. It has Numdah rugs, round and square, from a little under £5, and sheepskins (washable) as well as those Greek goatskins that glow whiter-than-white from £5.50. For kitchens and bathrooms and corridors they have fantastic Haiti rush-matting; you fit the oblong strips together, and they cost from 75p for a piece around 20″ × 30″. They used to have beautiful oval mats too—but they haven't been coming in of late although they're expected; maybe things haven't been the same in Haiti since Papa Doc died.

Quite a few butchers—even one in Moore Street—sell sheepskins. The Sheepskin Shop in Redmond's Hill has an amazing variety and Twomey's at 30 Bachelor's Walk is another rich source.

A bottle of Swift can transform the nastiest of old Turkey strip carpets into a piece of richly-jewelled and luxurious flooring. You buy carpeting from house auctions (the farther out of town, if you have a car, the cheaper : watch the papers) or from junk-shops like Mr George Monaghan's of Charlemont Bridge, or at the left-hand entry of the Daisy Market.

But if you're blessed with a willing landlord, you can do a lot more than all these cover-up operations : read on.

Painting the walls

makes an unbelievable difference to a room; you just won't believe it until you've tried it. You can lighten, warm, enrich and enliven the entire atmosphere with your choice of colour : you'll see. And if you are ready-equipped with a roller, two sizes of brush and a tray (from Brooks Thomas' home department or Dockrell's of South Great George's Street) as well as a pile of newspapers and a bottle of white spirits and paintstripper, you will be all ready to transform the mood of your room with a coat of paint for around £5 upwards.

Different paint firms are good for different colours. Crown have good strong simple ones, MacDonalds are good for yellows—buttery ones and sunflowery ones—and Robbialac are best for mix-it-yourself unusual shades like cinnamony browns and dusky pinks. You can generally coax the sales assistant into selling you an extra tube or two of colour if your Robbialac choice isn't quite strong enough for you. Eggshell is a strong, matte finish and I personally prefer it to gloss although it is not quite as tough. For sink areas you need Valspar enamel, or a polyurethane paint: these can take several days to dry, so see if you can do it at tea-time on a Friday, and then go home for the weekend. Or simply stay out, so as not to leave fingerprints all over. If you don't like enamel-gloss finish, you can get a matte washable one on things that take heavy wear, like chairs, by painting with ordinary water-based emulsion and then coating with several coats of polyurethane glaze.

Hints

1 If you're living in a small cramped room, you have the choice of trying to lighten it with white emulsion or a jolly, sunny yellow; or alternatively making it warm and cave-like with hazel-nut brown or magenta. Choose your colour to match its hoped-for character and be careful; it will affect your mood too. Who wants to get the Midnight Blues all day?

2 You can lower one of those totteringly high ceilings with a dark colour. I had successions of chocolate-brown ceilings because I discovered they had a psychologically-calming effect upon my peace of mind.

3 You can bring out fancy plasterwork in a different range of colours. For instance, I once had a fireplace with thrushes twittering away and butterflies fluttering all round the edge; the room was nearly all yellow so I mixed some of the left-over yellow with orange and red from the tubes and picked out the wild-life in varying shades on white. It looked all right, if I do say so myself.

4 For God's sake mix all the paint up in a big gallon can with an old stick before you start; a streaky effect is very grating to the eye. And you may need two coats to blot out whatever's underneath, so bring the dimensions of your room on a scrap of paper when you go to the shop and they'll tell you how much you need.

5 Remember to move as much as you can out of the room before you start; it makes it all much quicker if you're not tripping over mahogany wardrobes at any rate. Smother everything very carefully with newspapers, plastic sheets, old curtains and what-have-you. In fact where there are edges (between ceiling and wall, wall and floor) you'd do well to tack the old drapes to the skirting boards with drawing pins, and pin newspaper along the picture-rails with dress-making pins.

6 Wear clothes you don't give a damn about. If you haven't any, turn the ones you care the least about inside out, and scrub whatever paint falls on them before it dries out again. Otherwise you'll be too sad about your clothes to be happy with the room.

7 Look after your brushes so that you can use them again. Nothing is so infuriating as a brand-new perfectly good brush that is rock hard with paint and therefore unusable. If you've been using emulsion, hot soapy water and a rinsing is enough. For gloss, dunk in turps before rinsing and if necessary use paint-stripper.

8 Around window-frames, newspaper glued to the edges will make a nice clean line. But it's easy to scrape stray paint off glass with a knife blade, or a bit of fine sand-paper. For other edges, try a piece of cardboard held along the line with one hand while you paint with the other.

9 Have a damp cloth, either clutched in your other mitt or near to hand, so that you can quickly wipe whatever needs it.

10 Remember that colours always dry darker than you think they're going to; even brown can seem quite light and then very sombre when dry.

Other ways of covering walls

Wallpaper is sadly expensive, and a drag to apply well without lots of space and help. Lining paper, at under 50p a roll, will cover badly ruined ceilings; it is always cream colour—a rather nice non-colour in fact. You can get brown wrapping paper from wholesalers by the huge roll, for roughly £5. Hely's or Chamber's would sell you it, but for a smallish room you would only need about one quarter of the entire roll. It sounds odd but it's a beautiful warm colour with a nice softish texture: apply it like wallpaper. First measure the height of the room, and cut the number of lengths you will need; for this you need a simple knowledge of long division and a one-sided razor-blade.

Stretch the strips along your floor and paste them with Polycell; fold the strips into a succession of soft pleats and (here's where you need a friend) fit the pieces along the top first, smoothing the pleats out as you work your way down, ironing it all out with a soft brush; it always looks gluey and nasty until it dries. Be careful with the edges, and get it nice and straight, even if it means peeling it off again.

Sacking is fantastic as a wall-covering; it makes a good surface for pinning things on to, and is good for covering bubbly, damp-damaged walls. You can get it in natural colours from Goodbody's of 21 Earlsfort Terrace. It comes 6' wide and cost varies according to the closeness of the weave. You need several boxes of drawing pins to attach it, and it's a tricky operation because the sacking stretches a little and it's the kind of job that has to be done really well to look at all good.

Felt will cover unlovely patches and damaged doors and table tops as well. It also makes a great surface for pinning things on to if you're hindered by a no-posters-on-the-walls landlady. Arnott's stock it in a choice of widths and some gorgeous shades. You can glue it with Copydex, nail it with drawing pins or, more decorously, evenly-spaced brass up-

holstery tacks or—if it's for a table—fringe it with a
shading fringe and lay it on like a tablecloth.

Rugs are better than pictures; if you should come across
a really beautiful Numdah rug or inherit a Persian gem,
hang it on the wall with nails above the sofa or facing
the door.

Views

You can really get depressed if you have to stare at a
brick wall all day. I often wonder why the owners of brick
walls don't paint them with rainbow stripes, or the Gas
Board doesn't invite well-known artists to paint magnificent murals all over their sides. But they don't.

One thing you can do is line your windowsill with
gorgeous plants (see **Windowbox gardening** in the last
chapter). The other thing you can do is buy very fine
quality tissue paper from Browne and Nolan's of Dawson
Street and make yourself a sort of stained-glass window
by sticking shapes on, gluing them round the edges. You
can also paint on the glass with dilutable acrylic paints;
a palm-tree with a Technicolor sunset across Ringsend
gasworks might be quite alluring.

Or you can buy paper doilies to glue to the panes, or
even cut a delicate pattern out of folded white tissue paper
to paste on glass. So do not despair.

Lights

Lighting affects atmospheres dramatically (see **Lighting**
in the previous chapter). Good lampshades make a lot of
difference too; you can cover an existing shade with a very
fine flowered silk scarf, from a market or a sale, to cast
a rich antique glow over things. Or you can buy a
Japanese tissue-paper lantern from Prior Interiors of

Dawson Street: a 12″ size costs £1.15, a 36″ costs £7 and a 48″ jumbo costs (ouch) £14.50. They are much cheaper in the North or in England; they're cheaper still in Japan. But if you can't afford them, and you can't go that far, make your own. Buy an extra-large balloon for a few pence in Woolworth's and a packet of white tissue paper. Blow the balloon up and stick pieces of tissue on with flour glue. Let the balloon dry through well. Finally cut the mouth of the balloon off, and pick some holes in the other end. Whip the dead balloon out, press your new shade back into shape from inside, and fix over your light bulb with pieces of cotton or string.

Antique shades are found in junk-shops; they sometimes have really huge glass ones on chains. Ask Mrs Lee in the Francis Street corner if she has any on the balcony.

Oil-lamps of the decorous kind begin around £15 now, which is a lot. The Dublin Antique Brass Company have the nicest—and the dearest. The S.P.Q.R. often have beauties, too, in Sandymount Road. Candles are addictive; after candlelight you will only want harsh bulbs again for working with; for socialising, and meditating quietly candles diffuse the softest most thoughtful light. You can buy cedar-scented candles in the Viking Shop (South King Street, the Mercer Hospital end) or patterned ones in the Glencolumbkille Shop in Trinity Street, or Market Ireland, Grafton Street. The Bord Fáilte souvenir shop in Stephen Street, off South Great George's Street also has them, as do the Barrenhill Gallery out at Baily near Howth, Designs on You in Monkstown Road, Teddy's Boutique on the sea-front in Dún Laoghaire and the Dandelion Market which has a week-round walk-around shop in Stephen's Green as well as a street-market next-door beside the College of Surgeons on Saturdays and Sundays. The Country Shop at 23 St Stephen's Green near Baggot Street also has them. These are also the places to visit for lovely presents: fine hand-thrown pottery, silk-printed scarfs, rush table-mats, hand-woven tweed, Aran knits, turf paper-weights and crosses and the like. They are good just to look at, even when you can't afford to buy anything.

Floors—lino and planks

Nasty lino can be painted with lino-paint, and so can boards. Brooks Thomas in Sackville Place or at their new superstore on the Naas Road out in Bluebell will advise you here. It's surprising how tough painted boards could be if you did the job properly; I painted mine with ivory paint once which really lightened the room—but I didn't let it all dry properly so it had a pattern of heavy footprints. Don't you do the same. If you want to sand the boards to a smooth, natural colour hire a french polisher for the day: you can get them delivered and collected again by equipment hire firms like the Rathmines Supply and Hire Service at 15A Oakley Road, Dublin 6 (tel: 972102) who will hire you anything from a hammer drill to a Nilfisk suction vacuum cleaner from a couple of quid per day up, depending on what it is. Other hire companies advertise in the evening papers.

Once polished the boards are then varnished with polyurethane glazing (and it's a horrible messy sort of job; you can't walk anywhere on the floor for days) or slightly coloured with a pale translucent glaze like Translac, which comes in a nice red, blue, yellow, green or white as well as a variety of wood-colours to slightly tint the wood while showing off the grain. You can get it from Dockrells of South Great George's Street again.

Dye nasty carpets with carpet-dye from Associated Traders Ltd in Duke Street. They will provide you with a leaflet of instructions—and also a little booklet on how to tie-dye. You can do settees and deep armchairs the same way, and it will all be a lot easier than you thought.

Cleaning carpets is a matter of buying 1001 or Swift and having a persevering nature. With your junk shop carpet finds you will certainly need both in order to get past the century-old brown soup stains. You may, if it's strip-carpeting, also need a big carpet needle and linen thread to sew it all up.

Gilding the lily

If your flat is unfurnished, you will need to haunt junk-shops and auctions. Even if it's furnished, a little-thing-you-picked-up-for-a-silver-song will make something to swank about to your friends when you run out of other conversation.

Here's an imperfect list of the best junkshops in Dublin. It is imperfect and incomplete because they come and they—nowadays—very often go. I've only put in the really cheap ones for functional items, because if you can afford the lovely, lovely things in Butler's, Moles-worth Antiques or Heislip's in Galway, you will already know about them all.

The Quays have been the Mecca of junk-dealers (and I'm not saying 'junk' in a derogatory sense : I mean curious and fascinating second-hand items by the term) since the firm of Butler's first settled there in 1800. All the auction-rooms on Bachelor's Walk and Ormond Quay have weekly auctions; you have to cruise up and down past the windows regularly to view, and then come back later to make a bid in the auction itself.

Balfe's and Gately's at the end of Ormond Quay near Capel Street sell armchairs, bedsprings, side-boards, etcetera. I once got a vast *art nouveau* cabinet with seven mirrors from Gately's, plus a marble-topped toilet stand with a white china bucket and an olive-green velours bedspread, three bolsters and a lavender bag thrown in for a total £3.50. But that was three years ago.

Skelly's who hold auctions on Thursdays at Wellington Quay have old mattresses and springs and other fundamental items. So do Slowey's, near O'Connell Bridge on Bachelor's Walk. Often the article may need polishing, or a mass-pogrom on woodworms (buy a can of anti-worm from the hardware shop and inject the stuff firmly into every visible hole). But this only makes the finished article the more dear to you.

Matthew and Son, under Merchants' Arch, is now owned by Paddy Oman who also runs a brass-rubbing and polishing firm on the premises. It is well out of the 'junk' bracket and fair-to-medium expensive.

The Ha'penny Steps on the corner of Fleet Street and Merchants' Passage is another irresistible shop. In the same area is Sue Sweetman of Essex Street, good for stripped pine dressers and kitchen tables.

Junk around town. The most intriguing type of Dublin shop, the little jobbing establishment that springs up like the grass, and then gets trampled down again, is tending to die out. You have to keep your eyes peeled for them; there are some (nameless) ones left around the oldest corners of the city behind Bolton Street and Clanbrassil Street. They are where to go for your really functional pieces: brass beds, for instance, and bentwood chairs. They will be in rotten condition when you find them, so here's how you polish brass: with a lump of wire wool and a bottle of diluted domestic bleach, don your rubber gloves and scrub away. Then rinse and buy a small tin of fibre-soaked brass polishing pads. Shine.

Furniture can be vigorously stripped either with a Black and Decker drill fitted with a sanding attachment or with Nitromors rubbed into the corners (wear rubber gloves again). Then it is revarnished (even if it isn't stripped, it may like a revarnishing or at least a coating of linseed oil). When you're painting it, it's an idea to stand the legs of whatever it is on pieces of cork with pins in them, so that drips don't collect at the bottom and form a smudgy ridge. Keep a clean brush by to scrape the paint smooth on the under-edges of everything, so that they don't have paint-globs and drips along the sides either. You can glue transfers on for decoration or paint flowers with oil-paints —you can even cut them out, glue them on in a pattern and then protect with a couple layers of varnish.

Conway's at 14 Thomas Street have been selling interesting items for forty years. I found a complete extra-sized double-bed there for £6.50.

At Uncle Sam's in Francis Street Sam says the most valuable thing in his shop is himself. He is undoubtedly right, but you can often find happy little oddities among the roller-skates and plastic babies' baths.

Serendipity next door has a very pretty assortment of general bric-à-brac.

No 31 Upper Camden Street also has an endlessly fascinating collection. I found an exquisite inlaid Florentine cross for £1 here.

The Dandelion Market in St Stephen's Green varies wildly from the very smooth collector's piece to the newly-saved-from-Coolock-dump-with-a-few-coats-of-paint-thrown-on stuff. The former items tend to be in the week-day permanent shop, and the latter—plus lots of other goodies besides—in the weekend market beside it.

G. Monaghan's at 2 Charlemont Place may no longer be there by the time you read this book. He was one of the best, both for junk and for a friendly chat; he lives (lived) in one of those delicate and unappreciated little Georgian crescents by the canal and his treasure-trove is due to be rudely interrupted by a Compulsory Purchase Order any minute. Long may he survive it.

Nick Smyth at 68A Upper Rathgar Road has more assorted bric-à-brac.

Chelsea Antiques at Upper Leeson Street, past the fork on the left, is May Hannegal's shop with predictably unpredictable stock. You can also get sewing machines electrified here.

S.P.Q.R. in Sandymount Road is specially nice for odd pieces of nice china—but also for old Bibles, prints, lamps, the lot.

And again there are the Iveagh and the Daisy. And try the papers for sales and auctions.

Makeshift furniture

is easily made with concrete airbricks and planks of wood. Stack them at whatever depth and height you need them, for accommodating your books, papers, radiogram and table-lamps.

Airbricks only cost about 10p each from builder's providers like Kelly's of Thomas Street or O'Neill's of Oakley Road. You will need a car to collect them; I always 'borrowed' them from any friend who happened to be building a wall and then painted them white. Do not drop one on your toe. And do not carry more than one at a time if you value your back-muscles.

You can buy wood, and get it delivered, again from your nearest builder's provider. What they call 9-by-three-quarters-rough is best for shelving. Kelly's, O'Neill's and other timber-merchants are again your best bet. Look up your nearest under 'Timber' in the Golden Pages.

With sand-papering and a coat of varnish or paint, wooden mineral boxes like the kind you can buy from pubs or collect from the Shankill Wooden Box Company make great storage units. Stack them sideways to make bookshelves and lengthways to make open cupboarding for folded pullovers, geraniums-in-pots, lamps, magazines, whatever you like. Bracket them together and to the wall with what they call shamrock brackets (trefoil shaped brackets)—and screw into the wall with rawls for a tight safe join.

Making shelves isn't very hard either. Batons (or chocks) are the best support for the kind of shelving you stack in alcoves. The self-supporting kind, if your carpentry is good enough, make better jobs and they are easier to take away when you move. If you are both busy and rich—and lousy at carpentry to boot—you can buy screw-in metal brackets that you bolt your wood into at any desired height. Lenihans of Capel Street stock these; the wood is bought separately but altogether they could come to £10. Easier maybe to sign on for evening classes in joinery at your nearest 'Tec.

And now lean back and enjoy your flat. You deserve it.

APPENDIX 1 : BELFAST

Let me not be accused of Dublin snobbery for reducing Belfast to a sliver of printed pages. I know that it could fill a book of information in itself, that it has been consistently defamed by snotty-nosed southerners and isolated by its own defensiveness, and that at the moment of writing it is being devastated not by the Troubles alone, but also by the monstrous roadworks which the City Fathers deem right to drive straight through the middle.

I mean this section for visitors, and maybe the odd Queen's student. I would love to add to it, if there's any of it left and if I should get the chance.

Flats

Flats are very easy to find in Belfast these days. They are quite different in character from Dublin flats, being mostly lofty, Victorian and unfurnished. Around the Malone Road-Botanic Avenue-Ormeau Road-Lisburn Road-University Avenue they rise from £5 unfurnished to £7-£8 furnished per week; but in Belfast 'furnished' generally means a bed, a chair and a table—no delph, blankets or cutlery.

Around the Antrim Road area at the other side of the city they are £1 or so cheaper.

Flat-ads appear in the *Belfast Telegraph*; you can get at them first if you go to the *Telegraph* offices in York Street for an early afternoon edition.

There are also notice boards in the Union Building of Queen's University advertising flats to sub-let in the vacations; you can put up a card for 'Flat Wanted' there as well.

The rooms in Queen's Elms, the vast student hostels off the Malone Road, can be rented at half-price during the holidays: spartan but comfy and extremely good value.

Houses have not been so cheap in Belfast since the last war. A three-storey Georgian House in Joy Street has recently been bought for £600. Behind the University in Belfast 9, a red-brick Victorian family-house in decent repair may now be found for as little as £2,000-£3,000. This kind of price would make it possible for a group of people to buy one with a little money borrowed from kind benefactors: a group of very friendly, mutually understanding and solid young persons, that is. Renting an entire house is also easy, but landladies in the Righteous City are not keen on communes.

Temporary places. Again, a bed for the night is not difficult to find in Belfast; people are very hospitable— to their own. It is also well-supplied with hostels: the **Y.M.C.A.** near Queen's at Wellington Place (tel: 27231), the **Y.W.C.A.** for girls at 315 Malone Road (tel: 668347. Take 71 bus), the **Salvation Army** at 77 Holland Street (tel: 655861), the **Presbyterian War Memorial Hostel** at 46 Howard Street (tel: 26262/3) is excellent, though practically a hotel.

The Bed and Breakfast places are concentrated around Eglantine Road and Botanic Avenue; you should find a clean, comfy place for just under £1 per night.

Legal Aid

The Citizens' Advice Bureau in Bryson House at the top of Bedford Street will advise you free on your social and legal rights.

Family Planning

You will find advice and help at the Ulster Pregnancy Information Service (organiser : Mrs Lorna Goldstrom), at 198 Stranmillis Road, Belfast Tel: 667345)—and yes, it's legal here.

Furnishing

Your flat can be cheaply furnished by visiting a few auctions like Nicholl's in the Dublin Road, and Ross's of May Street. Paddy's Market off May Street to the other side used to be open on Friday mornings, but is liable to be interrupted by the troubles. There are some nice small junkshops around the Lisburn Road that display their wares (bentwood chairs, scrubbed tables and the like) on the pavement outside.

Foodshops

These do not generally stay open late, and most close for half-day on Wednesday. Spars of Fountain Street is the only one that does stay open on half-day near the centre. Supermac about 3 miles out in the Saintfield Road usually stays open certain evenings till 9. A lot of shops shut for lunch, and there are no little grotty corner shops that sell everything till pub-closing, the way there are in Dublin.

For Delicatessens there are the Chinese Wholesalers in Bedford Street (an emporium lined with tins of shark-fin soup and chow-chow, where the assistants play ping-pong all day long), Sawyer's of Castle Street, and Continental Fare at 27 Botanic Avenue, Belfast 7, have good selections.

Lunches

These are very good indeed if you just want a carton of soup and a couple of sandwiches to take to the nearest strip of park. There are lots of little places in the city centre that cater for that kind of snack—and Dublin could happily adopt the habit.

For a larger lunch try Gables at 1A India Street or The Whip and Saddle Room of the Europa if you have some spare time to be frisked and whisked by a mine-detector. McGlades' behind the *Belfast Telegraph* offices in York Street have good salad lunches in their upstairs lounge.

And Belfast enjoys some of the best home-baking in Europe of a no-nonsense and no-smothering-with-whipped-cream variety. There are good cake and bread shops, such as the Ormeau Bakery shops at Botanic Avenue and the Lisburn Road; there are scatterings of good tea-shops and coffee-bars like Isobeals in Wellington Street.

Cheap eating places

Good places surround, again, the Malone Road : The Graduate (130 University Street; tel : 33261), Smokey Joe's for a quick fry (again, the University Road), The Cobbles (43 Belmont Road, Belfast 4), and Ringo's ubiquitous van which stays around the Union Building till 2 or 3 in the morning and sells wowee cornish pasties; it manages to pop up everywhere.

The Nite-Bite at the corner of Victoria Street is good for take-away foods, but keeps getting raided for serving soldiers; it generally stays open late. Ken's Café just past the roundabout onto the Newtownards Road also has take-away chickens and chips, that sort of menu; it stays open till 4-5 am.

The good Chinese restaurants around Bedford Street and the city centre have taken to closing down early of late. But they still sell the native brew, Black Cat Cola, the strongest coke available in these islands.

Cheap household equipment

Cutlery and delph can best be found in Hogg's basement in Donegall Square, which often has oddments to sell cheaply. There is also, of course, Woolworth's in High Street.

Trendy household effects

Posters, nice carpets and lampshades can be found at Etcetera in Howard Street and at Interiors of Botanic Avenue; big stores like Anderson & MacAuley and Robinson & Cleaver in Donegall Place sell nicely-designed curtaining and the like. Spectrum at 27 Rosemary Street has luxury Casa Pupa carpets and other tantalising things.

Clothes

These are good and cheap, not just in the branches of Etam, C & A, Marks & Spencer and the British Home Stores but also in such places as the War On Want shop on Sandy Row (on the corner) and in the sprinkling of good jeans shops around Belfast 9. And you can, of course, get just about anything in Smithfield: it is especially good for old clothes, junk furniture, second-hand books and records as well as pet budgies, white mice —and contraceptives.

For good medium-priced boutique-type clothes there is Wallis' in Castle Place or Flair in Bedford Street.

137

Pubs

Students frequent the Club Bar, The Cobbles, The Eg., or even Hunters (where I was once thrown out for being an unaccompanied lady) depending on their scene.

The Crown Bar opposite Great Victoria Street station is still the best example of Belfast baroque in the city and Kelly's Cellars in Bank Buildings are still going strong.

All are closing early at the time of writing, and all are still—will nothing ever change this—closed on Sundays.

Entertainment

The Wellington Park Hotel has a disco on Wednesday nights. The Glenmacken Hotel has mainstream-modern jazz on Thursday nights, and a disco on Fridays and Saturdays (it is held in a converted stables in Hollywood). The Groomsport Hotel beyond Bangor has traditional jazz on Friday nights till 1 am. Pat's Bar up the Malone Road has folk music and the Imperial has a resident group as well.

Art Galleries are few but excellent: the Arts Council Gallery in Bedford Street and the Tom Caldwell Gallery in Bradbury Place. There is a good modern section to the Ulster Museum in the Stranmillis Road.

Theatres. The Lyric Theatre in Ridgeway Street is a compact, pretty modern theatre kept going by the Arts Council and the fiery determination of its founder, Mary O'Malley. It concentrates on classical drama and Yeats; but it also stages modern plays and new works.

The Arts Theatre and the Queen's Films Theatre as well as the Opera House are closed at the moment. They were talking of reopening this autumn however; for info, scan a copy of the *Telegraph* under 'amusements'.

Getting Away From It All which you may very well want to do. The Bellevue Zoo has a panoramic view of the Lough as well as the usual lions and flamingos. Take the Newtonabbey bus from Royal Avenue. The Ulster Folk Museum has a tiny cottier's cottage, and is good for counteracting a-Belfast-city-of-hate-and-tension type paroxysm. Get a Bangor bus and get off on the Bangor Road. For longer jaunts Ulsterbus will take you to Annamoe in the mountains of Mourne or the Giants' Causeway in craggiest northernmost Antrim. If things get really bad try Rathlin Island—and consult Ulsterbus on means of getting to the Ferry. If they get even worse, you could try throwing yourself to the lions of Benvarden near Dervock, Ballycastle.

APPENDIX 2 : CORK

Flats

Sunny, unexpected and Italianate, Cork is still hatching its first bedsitter explosion. And so there is no particular area you can point to for flats, and no modern blocks so far.

Students at University College, Cork have an internal accommodation bureau. They live in the Western Road—College Road—Connaught Road—Donovan's Road area. Many of the lodgings are just that—lodgings: there will be one room, without cooking facilities and with a shared bathroom for around £6 per week, perhaps including your evening meal as well as breakfast.

Sunday's Well is a slightly more expensive area, where you can find self-contained flats, and this is also true of Wellington Road and St Luke's Road; most of these are tall Regency houses on the tops of hills with unparalleled views for £8–£10 per week.

Montenotte is a laburnum-shrouded avenue of villas, some of which are converted into luxurious two-roomed flats. The surrounding roads will have not-quite-so-nice ones and the price range is £12–£15 per week.

The snag with all of these is that they are on weekly or monthly lettings; you can be chucked out at very abrupt notice. But you could try asking for a tenant's agreement. Even simply writing a letter to your landlord stating your terms will help, so long as he does not reply in disagreement, should it ever come to a court-case. The best security you can have is a lease, and flats with leases are best found in Cork through auctioneers.

Auctioneers charge the landlord, not you. But you are asked for a testimonial (from a 'respectable' older friend, who will tell them that you are really quite respectable too) and for a month's rent in advance, plus 5 per cent Stamp Tax. They sometimes ask for deposits too; £50 is usual.

The whole lot could easily come to a daunting £100. So if you are young and looking for a long-stay flat in Cork, it's probably better to get temporary digs while you look for a better place and save. Then take a nice, solid, secure lease on a good place from an auctioneers like Osborne, King and Megran's at 38 Marlborough Street, Cork (tel: 24077).

Houses can quite often be rented, either whole or divided into two halves. Young families who have gone to buy another home often sub-let their old semis in the suburbs; they charge £8–£10 per week.

Flat-hunting ads are best found in the *Cork Examiner*, 'Flats To Let' column, and 'Flats Wanted' section. There is also the *Echo*; you can get early editions from their offices at 95 Patrick Street, Cork.

Food

Markets. The best one is the Corporation Market which sells food and flowers only, and is held daily on Grand Parade. It's not all that much cheaper, but it *is* cheaper— especially if you go right down to the end stalls.

Delicatessens. Maher's of Lower Marlborough Street have good coffee and cold meats. Madden's of Bridge Street is a solid old family business where again you will find good cold meats, and a massive array of Hadji Bey's Turkish Delight—who used to have their own premises on MacCurtain Street before they were lamentably sold out. Smith's of 99 Patrick Street is another well-stocked and well-established grocer's.

Lunches. Maher's of Lower Marlborough Street again have an enormous variety of sandwiches and plates of salad. A great place.

The Green Room next door to the Opera House, and near the School of Art, has good, nourishing soup and tripe and onions. Something to suit every pocket as they politely say—meaning solid nosh plus extras.

Chinese restaurants are amazingly good in Cork; the Lucky Boat is one such, and will fill you well for 50p. But there are many more, up and around Patrick Street.

For social problems

If you are down and out, the Simon Community in John Street (tel: 53597) will see you right; they provide accommodation and friendly support to those undergoing hard times.

St Francis' Church helps young people in trouble : ask for Father Clarence who has helped drug-abusers and kids with other kinds of problems.

Legal aid. The Saint Vincent de Paul Society in Ozanam House, 2 Tuckey Street, has a branch of the Free Legal Aid Centre which will advise on problems to do with rent, arrests and the like. It does not represent you in court, but its student helpers are in the office on Wednesday nights to talk to anyone in trouble, from 8–10.30 pm. **Frances Hession** is the social worker who will help unmarried mothers and give advice on state aid (tel: 25126) but any girl concerned ought also to go to the Social

Welfare Department in Sheares Street for information on the benefits she is allowed.

Furniture

Colquay Market off Grand Parade has second-hand clothes, and the furniture you would need to furnish a flat or rented house. For furniture auctions try Hennessy's at 87 Main Street and Marsh's at 70 South Mall, Cork.

Kitchen Equipment

North Main Street and Shandon Street can fulfil just about any household need you might have in the way of hardware, electrical equipment stockists, etcetera. Cork Iron and Hardware have a large range, in North Main Street.

Clothes : Old

The Colquay Market by Grand Parade is the great place for relics of a bygone age, in clothes as much as furniture.

Pandora's Box in MacCurtain Street sometimes has good bargains in second-hand used clothes in excellent condition.

Cheap Clothes

Etam's in Patrick Street and Dunne's Stores almost opposite, for underwear, jerseys and socks.

Boutiques

Cork is full of them. Good ones are found in Paul Street (His & Hers, Hair and a couple more) and there is Trudy's in Academy Street, also Just Eve in Egan's of Patrick Street. A really nice boutique is Les Jumelles on Marlborough Street where the clothes are designed and made by the Doyle twins.

Entertainment

The lively Cork Arts Society holds its exhibitions on Lavitt's Quay.

Cork Choral and Orchestra have regular events.

The Everyman Theatre gives student reductions.

Cork Film Society continues to flourish, and

Cork Jazz Society holds Monday sessions at the Munster Hotel.

And Cork has a plethora of pubs where sing-songs spring up of themselves, and plenty of dance-halls as well.

Getting Away From It All is no problem at all when you have Youghal, Kinsale, the Beare Peninsula and the West Cork Gaeltacht there on your doorstep. You may be more interested in getting towards it all—but at any rate you are surrounded by lovely country there for the looking.

APPENDIX 3 : GALWAY

Ten years ago the flat situation in Galway City was very much a question of marvellously good value bed-and-breakfast in off-season Salthill.

Not now. Property is booming in Galway, and so is the population which has produced a sort of miniature Dublin muddle; four girls crammed in a room with beds as far as the eye can see, and stove dangerously near to the curtain, the ventilation practically nil and each paying at least £3 per week.

I'm glad about the population booming and the West awakening, but I think the time has come for a non-interested body—like UCG—to look around and see if some assembling of resources can't be mustered for the young country innocent who is so often exploited not only in his lodgings but also in his or her job as well. Pay has not risen in the cafés and hotels to parallel the rent increase, oh no.

Flats. There aren't all that many. What there are sprinkle the residential areas of Salthill and Newcastle, around the University Road. People on housing estates like Renmore often convert their garages; a bedsitter for one with kitchenette and bathroom like this would cost £6 upwards per week. University College, Galway, does distribute lists to its students here.

More expensive executive flats are found in the Crescent, Taylor's Hill and the White Strand Road. They are often in modern blocks, costing around £10–£12 per week. Hession is very often the agent for these.

The *Connaught Tribune* handles the ads for flats, and

to a lesser extent the *Galway Advertiser*. Get the country edition of the *Tribune* on Thursdays so that you can get at the ads a day earlier.

Digs are again in Salthill, and are often good value at around £5–£7 for half-board (that includes high-tea as well as breakfast). Again you will find the ads in the *Tribune*, or good digs may be recommended by someone else's landlady.

Chalets can sometimes be rented cheaply in winter, also holiday-type accommodation. The danger here is that they either suddenly become doubly expensive around June or you get thrown out to make way for the summer visitors. There's little security attached to them—but they can make cheap, cosy winter-accommodation.

Legal aid

Again Ozanam House (the St Vincent de Paul Society) in St Augustine Street, tel: Galway 3233, houses a branch of the Free Legal Advice Centre. The FLAC helpers are at home to talk to those with legal problems on Tuesday evenings 7.30–9.30 pm.

Social problems

The Galway Social Services Centre operates in St Francis Street, Galway (tel: Galway 3581).

Jobs

There are plenty a-going, both temporary and part-time in hotels and restaurants that cater for the summer crowd. But beware of long hours and rock-bottom pay; there is a tendency here to make slave-labour out of young people coming up from the country. Not everywhere of course.

Clothes

Of a basic kind: underwear, socks, jumpers—you can try old reliable Dunne's Stores in Eyre Square and the Blackrock Stores in Shop Street; there has been a rumour that the latter is closing down, however. But they are best for old-fashioned cheap button-down vests for you to dye or tie-dye at home. For jeans the Salthill Stores out in Salthill have a good, cheap, teenage collection.

For trendier stuff: the Salthill Stores again, and Madge's in High Street with Trudy's almost opposite. There is also the Blue Cloak in Abbeygate Street, well worth a look. You see lots of little signs up in the High Street area advertising dressmakers and even knitters and crochet-makers. Great opportunities for wild imaginations and ingenuity here: even if the usual clothes in the shops tend to be conservative.

Leather can be bought by the hide in a little shop on Prospect Hill if you want to make handbags, belts and weskits.

Galway City is well served by tiny little drapers' shops, lovely for poking around for old material that is ideal for patchwork, ganseys that Galway fishermen used to wear, wellington boots and plimsolls—and of course, hand-crocheted lace, beautiful on long, silky dresses.

Furniture

For second-hand stuff that you can afford, Tolco's in Lower Cross Street is a good place. There is also Silkes on Munster Avenue, and the pawn shop on High Street. If you need to furnish an entire house, try Dempsey's Auction Rooms on Prosperous Hill.

Kitchen Equipment

Try Knocktons' in Shop Street, also Corbett's farther

up; MacDonagh's in Merchants' Row as well. Woolworth's in Eyre Square is good for electrical equipment and the like.

Decorous touches. Away from the purely functional, the new Moon's has nice things in tableware and fabrics. It is fairly pricy, but worth it if you want to own such things as the hand-thrown Connemara pottery with a soft greeny-blue glaze.

Entertainment

slumps dramatically in winter with the tourist season. But try O'Reilly's (the Foster Arms) in Foster Street which has singing about three nights a week.

Jackson's is another singing pub which caters for Mervue Estate; and for local talent there is the Manhattan on the corner of Raven Terrace in the Claddagh—which has a great pianist and where you are invited to burst into song yourself.

Getting away from it all

You are surrounded by great boltholes of nature where you can escape; CIE in Eyre Square will help. The boat to the Aran Islands leaves from New Docks for (at the time of writing) £3.50 return. But Galway is a marvellous city, and will stay marvellous so long as they don't keep pulling chunks down in an effort to make it the bog Boom City.